Living a Liturgical Spirituality

Journeying Daily with CHRIST

JOYCE ANN ZIMMERMAN, CPPS

LITURGY TRAINING PUBLICATIONS

Nihil Obstat
Rev. Mr. Daniel G. Welter, JD
Chancellor
Archdiocese of Chicago
December 22, 2021

Imprimatur
Very Rev. Robert G. Casey
Vicar General
Archdiocese of Chicago
December 22, 2021

The *Nihil Obstat* and *Imprimatur* are declarations that the material is free from doctrinal or moral error, and thus is granted permission to publish in accordance with c. 827. No legal responsibility is assumed by the grant of this permission. No implication is contained herein that those who have granted the *Nihil Obstat* and *Imprimatur* agree with the content, opinions, or statements expressed.

LIVING A LITURGICAL SPIRITUALITY: JOURNEYING DAILY WITH CHRIST © 2022 Archdiocese of Chicago: Liturgy Training Publications, 3949 South Racine Avenue, Chicago, IL 60609; 800-933-1800; fax: 800-933-7094; email: orders@ltp.org; website: www.LTP.org. All rights reserved.

This book was edited by Timothy A. Johnston. Michael A. Dodd was the production editor, and Matthew B. Clark was the designer and production artist.

Cover art: *Hallelujah* by Mike Moyers © 2013, mikemoyersfineart.com. Used with permission.

26 25 24 23 22   1 2 3 4 5

Printed in the United States of America

Library of Congress Control Number: 2022931800

ISBN: 978-1-61671-676-9

LSJ

CONTENTS

ABBREVIATIONS   IV

INTRODUCTION   V

1. PASCHAL MYSTERY UNRAVELED   1

2. LITURGY UNLEASHED   12

3. LITURGICAL SPIRITUALITY UNCOVERED   26

4. DISCIPLESHIP EMBRACED   47

CONCLUDING REMARKS   61

APPENDIX: SPIRITUALITY OF LITURGICAL MINISTERS   63

    ASSEMBLY   64

    PRESIDER   67

    DEACON   70

    ACOLYTE   73

    LECTOR   75

    EXTRAORDINARY MINISTER OF HOLY COMMUNION   77

    LITURGICAL MUSICIAN   79

    MINISTER OF HOSPITALITY   82

    SERVICE MINISTER   85

ABBREVIATIONS

CCC   *Catechism of the Catholic Church*, 1994

GIRM   *General Instruction of the Roman Missal*, 2010

LG   *Lumen gentium*, Vatican II, "Dogmatic Constitution on the Church," 1964

NRSV   New Revised Standard Version of the Holy Bible

SC   *Sacrosanctum concilium*, Vatican II, "Constitution on the Sacred Liturgy," 1963

Introduction

Why? Why? Why? Parents of small children and anyone who has interacted with small children know that this question is incessantly asked. Why do I have to go to bed now? Why do I have to eat my broccoli? Why can't I go over to my best friend's house to play? And on and on. But small children are not the only ones who ask why questions. Adolescents want to know why they must go to Mass on Sunday. College students want to know why they must check in with parents regularly. Young adults want to know why they can't get a better job. Parents ask why they are so exhausted all the time. The elders ask why the time goes by so quickly. And on and on. Why questions help us to understand better the life unfolding around us. They help us to be clearer about our purpose in doing what we do. They help us delve more deeply into our motives. Sometimes why questions are in the back of our minds even when we are not specifically asking the question.

Obviously not all why questions are equally important to ask or even answer. The answer to why do I have to eat broccoli has far less import than the answer to why do I have to go to Mass on Sunday. The more weight a why question has, the more imperative it is that we ask it and pay attention to the answer. This book is really about asking a why question, and probably the most important one any of us can ever ask. The question: Why is it so important to live a liturgical spirituality? There is an obvious answer: So we can get to heaven. But asking this why question has far more depth and richness than even thinking about the glory of our ultimate destiny. Asking this question has to do with understanding better the life in Christ we choose to live, being clearer about the purpose of the choices we make every day and uncovering the motives that push us forward toward greater joy and happiness.

Choosing to live a liturgical spirituality shapes the very way we live. "A way to live" is a simple definition for spirituality. There are many distinct Christian spiritualties — for example, Benedictine, Franciscan, Ignatian, Marian, or Eastern. Many people have found great spiritual help in the guidance of these particular spiritualties. These and many other spiritualties within the Catholic Church share a number of Gospel values; at the same time, they each have very specific emphases. The Second Vatican Council's *Sacrosanctum concilium* (SC) asserts that liturgy is the source (fount) and summit of the whole Christian life (see SC, 10). In *Lumen gentium* (LG), the council stated the same thought, but about the Eucharist (see LG, 11). Thus the Council teaches us that our Christian living—our daily journey with Christ—flows from our celebration of liturgy and brings us back to the celebration of liturgy. Liturgy is the heart, the nourishment, the inspiration for who we are and all that we do. Eucharist is the answer to that most important why question we can ask. At least that is ideally what liturgy is. Liturgical spirituality and our daily living of it brings the ideal to a very practical awareness that can be identified, measured, critiqued.

Living a liturgical spirituality reminds us that liturgy does not end when the ritual is concluded. For example, when we are dismissed at the end of Mass, we do not simply leave church and get on with life. The celebration of Mass transforms us; it is a radical encounter with the risen Christ. Therefore, the dismissal from Mass invites us to take leave from the ritual transformed and renewed in the Spirit, ready to embrace Gospel-living in ever fresher ways. The more fervently we celebrate liturgy, the more eagerly do we embrace the mission of Jesus in cooperating with him to bring salvation to all. To live liturgical spirituality is to live a mystery: the very mystery of Jesus' saving, loving life. To live liturgical spirituality is to embrace the richness and depth of this mystery. It is to make it our own.

Each chapter in this book on liturgical spirituality responds to a different why question about living a liturgical spirituality by journeying daily with Christ. Chapter 1 responds to the question: Why be so taken up with the saving mystery of Christ, and why does that have anything to do with our daily living and the choices we make? Chapter 2: Why does liturgy enact the saving mystery of Christ in the here and now, in our very messy daily living? Chapter 3: Why does choosing to make liturgical spirituality the center of our lives affect who we are and what we do? Chapter 4: Why is liturgical spirituality demanding, but at the same time encouraging, in that we are not alone in this way of living? The appendix also answers a why question: Why does each of the particular liturgical ministries help us see the many ways that liturgical spirituality can be expressed in our daily living? At the conclusion of each chapter is an opportunity to review and reflect on what struck the reader in the chapter, moving one toward grasping concretely all that is involved in living a liturgical spirituality.

Lots of why questions! The exciting part of all this is that even after we have delved into all these questions, we will have grasped only a tiny bit of the mystery of Christ's saving deeds. This is not meant to be a discouraging admission. It is a bold statement asserting that each day of our lives gives us a remarkable opportunity to enter into the depth of God's mystery of love for us. In turn, the more perfectly we are able to live liturgical spirituality, the more profoundly we ourselves fall in love with God. Ultimately, then, liturgical spirituality is about falling in love; it is about inviting us to love God, each other, and self ever more deeply. It is also about drawing us to celebrate, by each breath we take, the depth of this God-human love relationship. May Christ dwell in our "hearts through faith, as [we] are being rooted and grounded in love" and experience the great joy of "the breadth and length and height and depth" of the "love of Christ" (Ephesians 3:17–18, NRSV).

1

PASCHAL MYSTERY UNRAVELED

It hardly seems possible that prior to the Second Vatican Council (1962–1965), the term *paschal mystery* was not part of our everyday religious language. Most Christian people today would at least have heard of the term, even if they do not have a clear idea of what it is all about. Sadly, too many people still have little idea about the meaning of this mystery for them. Simply put, the paschal mystery concerns the saving events of Jesus: his becoming incarnate in the Virgin Mary, his life and ministry, teaching and preaching, healing and caring, death and resurrection, ascension into heaven, and sending the Holy Spirit to dwell within us. The challenge for us is to move those saving events beyond past historical occurrences and to begin grasping the paschal mystery as that into which we are immersed at baptism, that which we celebrate at every liturgy, and that which we live each day. The paschal mystery is a mystery because love is a mystery. Our unraveling the paschal mystery leads us deeper into the love relationship between God and us humans. Love can never be exhausted; it only grows deeper and deeper. As our love for God grows deeper through our participation in the paschal

> The paschal mystery concerns the saving events of Jesus: His becoming incarnate in the Virgin Mary, his life and ministry, teaching and preaching, healing and caring, death and resurrection, ascension into heaven, and sending the Holy Spirit to dwell within us.

mystery, we grow deeper and deeper in the Life that God so generously and abundantly offers us.

We begin our reflection in this chapter with the paschal mystery as the mystery of salvation; then we consider how we are first and continually immersed in this mystery; next we think about how the mystery unfolds as a dynamic rhythm characterizing our daily living in Christ; and finally, we ponder how this mystery aptly opens us to fruitful Gospel living.

The Saving Mystery of Christ

As we listen to the proclamation of the Gospel during the Liturgy of the Word, or if we take the time to read prayerfully through one of the Gospels, we cannot help but notice that healing is one of the primary actions that Jesus does during his public ministry. Word gets around quickly! It seems like wherever Jesus goes, crowds follow him, eagerly anticipating that some healing might take place. How tiring this ministry must have been for Jesus. And, indeed, Luke's Gospel tells us that after healing a leper, Jesus went off by himself to pray and, no doubt, also get some rest and just recoup his energy, purpose, and mission (see Luke 5:12–16). Why did Jesus heal so much? The simple answer is that there were as many sick people then as there are today. Healing is Jesus' most often performed miracle; in fact, in one way or another, all his miracles were healings. He healed hunger with the multiplication of the loaves and fishes; he healed from death by returning Lazarus to life; he healed the pain and alienation of sin by forgiveness; he healed, he healed, he healed. Why? Because Jesus was the compassion, mercy, and love of the Father personified in human form. His healing was (is) a pure act of love. Further, Jesus' healing ministry is indicative of why he came: to bring us salvation.

All too often when we hear the word *salvation* we limit its meaning to "being saved from our sins." While this is certainly true, salvation has a much broader and richer significance. The root of the Hebrew word meaning "salvation" is *Yesha'*. Derivative words with which we are familiar include *Joshua, Hosea, Isaiah, Jesus,* and *hosanna*. Originally, *salvation* did not have a religious context at all. It meant a "broadening" or "enlarging"; it meant the creation of space in the community for life and conduct. This space was freeing or liberating; the space rendered help or protection. Eventually, salvation began to take on religious meaning and came to indicate wholeness, health, and well-being (a familiar derivative is the word *salve*, an ointment used to heal a wound).

With the advent of Jesus, salvation was refined even more to mean the establishment of God's end-time reign, coming to wholeness and completion, and entering into the fullness of God's Life. Jesus revealed to us a far greater sign than physical healing. His saving work included the forgiveness of sins, liberation from evil, and establishing a relationship with God. Jesus' saving work also reminds us that salvation is a divine initiative and election—that is, God begins and chooses us for salvation. Salvation is the work of God's mercy, and not solely a matter of our good choices and actions. We do not "earn" salvation. Rather, we are called to live as Jesus taught us; we live the Gospel. Salvation is not a matter of doing someone a good deed, and then getting points in heaven for it. Yes, doing good for others is essential. However, caring for others is essential not because we get points in heaven, but because we are responding to Jesus' commandment of love. When we love another and do good for another, we are growing in our relationship with God, others, and self. We are growing in our capacity to live as Jesus did.

Jesus' saving mission was fundamentally a healing mission. All his healings were a sign of the in-breaking of salvation; the in-breaking of God in human history. He healed to show us why we would choose to follow him: Because that is how we grow in our relationship with God, that is how we deepen God's Life within us, that is how we journey daily with Christ. What was required for Jesus to heal? First, there must be an encounter with Jesus; the one desiring to be healed must seek Jesus, be open to his divine will, be filled with hope that Jesus desires our wholeness, and be willing to receive Jesus' healing touch. Often Jesus remarks that a sick person was healed because their faith saved them (for example, see Luke 8:43–48). Faith in this context is not an adherence to a set of doctrines. Rather, faith is acceptance of Jesus and living the Gospel; faith is saying yes to God's will. Faith is an action. It is a process of relationship rather than a single act. The narrative about the woman caught in adultery is very telling (see John 8:3–11). This is a parable loaded with lessons. Not only does Jesus turn judgment around, so that those accusing the woman of adultery are led to facing their own sinfulness and even admitting it by walking away, but also, after the accusers have left, Jesus dismisses the adulterous woman with the clear admonition to sin no more. The healing was much more than saving the woman from a not-very-pleasant death. The healing was a saving act that changed lives. And we all know that change is a process, rarely coming about suddenly. Just so, salvation is a process of lifelong learning that we only come to wholeness and fulfillment, when we surrender ourselves to the Life that Jesus offers. The surrender is a lifelong process of relationship. It begins with our baptism.

Baptism and Our Participation in Christ's Saving Mystery

Some of us tend to limit our understanding of liturgy only to the liturgical enactment, the actual liturgical celebration. We go to liturgy and we are dismissed from it. That's it. Now we get on with our daily living. In fact, this is not (or ought not be) the case. True, liturgy is enacted during a ritual that has a beginning and an end. But that is not all there is to liturgy. The beginning and end of liturgy, in fact, is the beginning and end of our life with God. This begins at baptism and ends with our participation in the eternal, heavenly liturgy. In other words, liturgy is a lifelong celebration of God's faithfulness and goodness to us. It is a celebration of our extraordinary privilege to share in God's divine Life. This extraordinary privilege is first ritualized at our baptism.

Baptism is not a once-and-for-all yes that either our parents/godparents uttered (if we were baptized as infants) or we ourselves uttered (if we were baptized as an older child or adult). Our whole life is to be a continual yes to God's will, God's love, God's Life coursing within us. As Jesus' conversation with Nicodemus tells us, we are to be reborn into God's Life (see John 3:1–8). Through rebirth in the Holy Spirit we receive God's Life. The baptismal waters are Life-giving. That Life remains within us so long as we never reject it, never decisively turn from God, never completely sever our relationship with God.

In addition to this Life-giving gift of baptism, there is also a death-dealing gift of baptism. St. Paul tells us that when we are plunged into the baptismal water, we die with Christ (see Romans 6:3–4). The old self dies so that the new self that emerges from the baptismal water is united with Christ in his risen Life. In baptism we are united with Christ in his death and resurrection. Just as Jesus passed from death to the new Life of resurrection, so do we pass from death to new Life in Christ through baptism. Christ gives us a share in his risen Life, and we in turn give ourselves over to living his Life through our words and actions. Baptism is a kind of first step in a lasting and growing friendship built on a mutual exchange of self-giving.

The "ongoingness" of baptism is nothing less than our participation in and fidelity to the saving mystery of Christ. The initial yes to God made at baptism is continually ratified through the choices we make in our daily living. Each yes we make to Gospel living is a fresh embrace of our baptismal commitment. Liturgically and practically, we say yes at baptismal liturgies throughout the year when the whole gathered assembly is invited to renew their own baptismal vows. This renewal is also a crucial moment at the Easter Vigil or the Easter Sunday liturgies when the assembly of the baptized is invited to renew their baptismal vows. This renewal of vows is not a matter of starting over, as if we somehow erased the commitment we made. No, the renewal of baptismal vows is a reminder to us that our lifelong commitment to be identified with Christ in his life, death, and resurrection is very real and carried out in the everyday choices we make about how we live.

So much of Jesus' ministry was characterized by his self-giving. This is evident in all his actions, whether he was preaching and teaching, healing and bringing to wholeness, or forgiving and showing mercy. Jesus gave of his own self in all these actions, sometimes very physically as when he touched the blind man's eyes with mud made with his saliva (see John 9:6–7) or when he did not shrink from physically touching a leper in the healing process (see Matthew 8:1–3). Jesus' greatest act of self-giving is the ongoing sharing of his very Body and Blood in the Eucharistic sacrifice. As those baptized into Jesus' saving mystery, we are called to continue in our own lives Jesus' self-giving. We may not heal blindness with mud made from our saliva, or we may not physically touch a leper, but we surely can respond in very personal ways of self-giving to the myriads of needs we come across each day.

Sometimes we might think that following Jesus means doing big, obvious, hit-me-over-the-head good deeds. In fact, most of us humbly live out the Gospel by doing all the little things in daily life with the kind of compassion and care and love that Jesus would bring to situations. A smile at the grocery store cashier who seems frazzled, a word of encouragement to a friend who seems disheartened, a phone call to an elderly relative living alone, a warm embrace of a young child who seems disconnected, or an offer of a helping hand to an over-burdened parent are all little but so important ways of participating in the saving mystery of Christ. These are ways we say yes to our baptismal call to bring the risen Christ's Presence to all we meet. Any act of self-giving is truly an act of risen Life. Self-giving/risen Life: This is the rhythm of Christian living, the rhythm of the paschal mystery unraveling in all we do.

PASCHAL MYSTERY AS A RHYTHM OF LIVING

As we noted above, we are plunged into Christ's saving mystery at baptism; we are plunged into Christ's paschal mystery. Unravelling this mystery to access its deep richness is no easy task, but it surely is not impossible. Let us explore further this mystery by looking at the two words themselves.

The actual origins of the word *paschal* are obscure. Most scholars trace its meaning to the Hebrew word for Passover, *pesach*. We know the story of the Passover: When Moses was sent to the Pharaoh to set the Israelites free, Pharaoh refused to let them go. So began the ten plagues of Egypt. The last plague (see Exodus chapter 11) was God's slaying the firstborn of all in the land. But to save the firstborn of the children of Israel, God (through Moses) instructed the people to eat a meal before departing from Egypt (see Exodus chapter 12). The entrée for this special meal was to be a year-old, unblemished male lamb (see Exodus 12:5). The lamb was to be slaughtered and some of its blood was to be smeared on the doorposts and lintels (see Exodus 12:7) of each Israelite house. This blood would be a sign that when God strikes down the firstborn in Egypt, God will "pass over" the houses marked with the blood of the Passover lamb (see Exodus 12:13). This is the Passover meal still celebrated by the Jewish people each year to commemorate their "passing" over from slavery to freedom.

Shifting now to *paschal* in a Christian context, Jesus is the new Passover Lamb by whose blood we "pass over" from the slavery of sin to new Life in Christ. From what does Jesus "pass over"? He passed over from death to resurrection, from this life on earth to risen Life and taking his place at the right hand of his Father. Built into the word *passover* is a rhythm between death and Life, between sin and innocence, between being alienated or conformed to Christ. Our "passover" includes a promise and a hope: A promise of new Life and a hope that one day we will be united with the risen Christ in his eternal glory.

Now let us look at the second word of *paschal mystery*. A mystery is not the same thing as a problem. Science and reason can solve a problem, given time and perseverance. A mystery, by its very nature, is beyond solving because its depth can never be exhausted, and it does not have a single explanation. In a Christian context, mystery is revealed by God and is primarily known by faith. This does not mean that we are incapable of studying the meaning of a mystery or what it reveals. But our grasp of mystery is a gift of God. We can know something about a mystery, but not all there is to know. A mystery can be described in many ways, which is the beauty of it. For example, life is a mystery; we know something of the meaning of life as a biological entity (the heart is beating, the brain is functioning, all bodily systems are a "go") but yet, for all the advances in medical science, much about the human body and its life still eludes us. From a spiritual viewpoint, life is even more of a mystery. We know we can enrich our spiritual lives, we know when our spiritual lives are fulfilling, and we know when there is something not quite right with us spiritually but yet, for all our prayer and reflection about God and our relationship with the Divine, much about our spiritual life also eludes us.

The paschal mystery describes the saving mission of Jesus. We are plunged into that saving mission through our baptism. But as we mentioned above, baptism is not simply a ritual moment unfolding in chronological time, but it is an ongoing commitment to live as Christ lived. Since the paschal mystery plays between two poles of dying and rising, we might think of living the paschal mystery as a rhythm, a cadence. We live between dying and new Life, between self-emptying and fullness, between surrender and utter freedom, between self-giving and deepening of love, between taking up our cross daily and saving our Life (see Luke 9:23–24).

We human beings tend to focus on the negatives in our lives—on what is bothering us and on what is not quite right with things. The paschal mystery invites us to recognize that however the "dying" comes in our daily living—no matter the difficulties we experience and sufferings we endure—it always opens onto new Life when we place these challenges in the context of our following Christ faithfully. This is a tremendous source of hope and confidence! Indeed, in the very dying (self-giving, self-emptying, surrendering) is already the rising (fullness, freedom, deepening of love) because in the dying we are conforming more perfectly to Jesus and his life of self-giving. The hope we receive by being conformed to Jesus and his saving mission is a hope borne out of knowing that dying is not all there is to Jesus' saving mystery. Faithful living of the paschal mystery leads to our eternal glorification, our eternal union with the Life of the risen Christ. This hope is the source of the joy we experience when we know we have said yes to some opportunity to live the Gospel more fully. Paschal mystery has everything to do with everyday living!

Paschal Mystery and Everyday Living

There is yet another thread to unravel in coming to a deeper grasp of the paschal mystery and our participation in it. Through baptism we are grafted onto Christ and become members of his Body. Because of baptism, we can say of ourselves and others that we are the Body of Christ. Our everyday living of the paschal mystery is our everyday living as Christ lived—living as faithful disciples. This would be a daunting challenge except that we are never alone in this lifelong journey. We not only have Christ as our Good Shepherd, who leads us along our life journey, but we also have each other, members of the Body of Christ. What we do for one, we do for others. What others do, they do for us. All of us together are building up the Body of Christ to full stature (see Ephesians 4:13).

It is sometimes said that God sent the Son to suffer and die for our sins. While there is certainly some measure of truth in this statement, it is really a limiting way to consider Jesus' life and mission. God the Father certainly did not send the divine Son to dwell among us just to suffer and die. What good father would wish suffering and death on a son? Jesus' Father sent him to show us the way to his Father. If we know Jesus, who is the way, the truth, and the life, then we know his Father (see John 14:6–7). We know who Jesus is through Scripture, Tradition, and through over two millennia of baptized Christians living as Jesus did. We know who Jesus is through the goodness of each other. We know who Jesus is through seeking him in all those we meet and all things we do.

> Our everyday living of the paschal mystery is our everyday living as Christ lived—living as faithful disciples.

Jesus died at the hands of some of the Jewish leadership because he challenged their way of living and leading. Some of the leadership put human laws ahead of God's Law (see Mark 7:1–8). Jesus did not come to abolish the Law of God (see Matthew 5:17–18); he came to fulfill it. The fulfillment of God's Law is summed up in the two great commandments, as Jesus said to the Pharisees (see Matthew 22:34–40): We must love God above all, and we must love each other as ourselves. Jesus showed us what this love looks like by the way he lived: total self-giving, total obedience to his Father's will, total surrender of even his life in order to be faithful to the saving mission his Father asked him to fulfill.

There must be a rhythm in our own daily living of the paschal mystery. This rhythm unfolds in a number of ways. It is expressed in the choices we make daily in the myriad ways of self-giving we embrace. Each time we reach out to another in love, we are living the rhythm of the paschal mystery. For in self-giving we are uniting ourselves with Christ's self-giving, and so also share in his risen Life. Sometimes we are not even aware of this rhythm happening: the automatic smile in response to another, the unthinking helping hand reached out to someone burdened, or the unspoken commitment to be present to those who are alone and ailing. Each of these are all ways we give to others, ways we live the paschal mystery.

Another rhythm of the paschal mystery unfolding in our lives occurs with our choice to find a right balance between prayer and action. We can become so busy with so many responsibilities and activities that we become too tired to pray, become too preoccupied to think of God (even in such a simple way as uttering a prayer of gratitude for the moving traffic), and become too bogged down in exhaustion that we cannot focus even for a few minutes on the God who blesses us with all good.

Yet another rhythm of the paschal mystery unfolding in our lives is the challenge to take care of ourselves in mind, body, and spirit. The paschal mystery's demand to be self-giving does not remove the obligation that we take good care of ourselves. Each of us needs "down" time. We need to learn to appreciate silence, to sit quietly in rest, to choose to eat healthy foods, to exercise, and so on. We need to balance pain with laughter, activity with reflection, and doing with marveling at the gracious being God has created us to be.

In the introduction, the question we posed to be addressed in this first chapter was, Why be so taken up with the saving mystery of Christ, and why does that have anything to do with our daily living and the choices we make? We are taken up with the saving mystery of Christ because his mystery is our mystery to be lived through our baptismal commitment. Baptism's yes to God is a yes to being Christ for all we meet each moment of each day. As we ourselves grow in God's Life, as we ourselves grow in the health and wellbeing that is salvation, we are impelled to share this Good News with others. The saving mystery of Christ describes who we are and how we live. Indeed, the saving mystery of Christ has everything to do with our daily living.

We turn now to the next chapter, where we are filled with wonder at God's goodness in providing us with all the means to be nourished and strengthened. In liturgy we ritually enact the paschal mystery truth of Gospel living.

Chapter 1: To Review and Reflect

The saving mystery of Jesus is made visible in healing and loving and caring relationships.

- I need to be healed of . . .
- The relationships I most treasure are . . .
- I bring others salvation when I . . .

The paschal mystery is a rhythm of dying and rising, of self-emptying and Life-receiving.

- For me in my life, the various threads of the paschal mystery to be unraveled are . . .
- I am aware of being plunged into the paschal mystery at my baptism when . . .
- The rhythm of my daily living might be described as . . . What I need to do to become more mindful of the rhythm of the paschal mystery in my daily living is . . .

From this chapter, I wish to remember . . .

2

Liturgy Unleashed

*L*iturgy is a word that has only come into the everyday vocabulary of the followers of Christ since *Sacrosanctum concilium* (SC) was promulgated on December 4, 1963, by the Second Vatican Council. Over the decades SC has guided and energized the ongoing liturgical renewal. Unfortunately, even so many years after the council, the word *liturgy* has tended to become synonymous with Mass. It is certainly true that Mass is liturgy, but that is not the only liturgical celebration. The word *liturgy* can have a very specific meaning, as well as a very broad-reaching meaning.

Documents of the Church that address various liturgical topics tend to be very explicit about that to which they refer. This specific, *official* use of liturgy includes the celebration of the seven sacraments and the Liturgy of the Hours (or Divine Office). Probably many of us need to remind ourselves that even our "private confession" to a priest is really and truly liturgy. As such, this seemingly very private act of confession is still a celebration of the whole Church. How can this be? It is so because all liturgy is an act of the whole Church celebrating the saving mystery of Christ. This brings home to us the importance of viewing ourselves as members of the Body of

> All our living not only can be, but ought to be paschal mystery living; all our everyday living can be a kind of liturgy when we are faithful to the dynamic rhythm of the paschal mystery as self-emptying and Life-receiving.

Christ. When some members of the Body of Christ celebrate liturgy, all the members celebrate.

Nonetheless, even when broadening our understanding of the meaning of liturgy beyond Mass (how many people refer to it) to include all the sacraments and the Liturgy of the Hours, we still haven't exhausted an adequate understanding of liturgy. Two other ways to expand our grasp of the depth-meaning of liturgy is that liturgy enacts the paschal mystery, and that liturgy unfolds in our everyday paschal mystery living. In other words, all our living not only can be, but ought to be paschal mystery living; all our everyday living can be a kind of liturgy when we are faithful to the dynamic rhythm of the paschal mystery as self-emptying and Life-receiving. Let's further unpack this broader approach to liturgy.

Liturgy Enacts the Paschal Mystery

Above we referred to living the rhythm of the paschal mystery. What is this rhythm? It is the back and forth, the interaction, the creative tension between dying and rising, between self-giving and risen Life, between this life and the fullness of the next Life that awaits those who are faithful to the Gospel. The paschal mystery unfolds between two never-ending poles of self-emptying and Life-receiving. We emphasize that these poles unleash a creative tension, because we can never ignore the truth of either pole in our daily living, nor only live one of the poles exclusively. This rhythm describes our daily life in Christ; it also describes a rhythm that unfolds in liturgy.

Every liturgy (as celebration of the sacraments and Liturgy of the Hours) has a four-fold structure. In the case of the seven sacraments, that structure is Introductory Rites, Liturgy of the Word, Liturgy of the Sacrament, and Concluding Rites. In the case of the Liturgy of the Hours, the fourfold structure is Introductory Rites, Psalmody, Intercessions, and Concluding Rite. Of course there are many other elements that flesh out this fourfold structure in each different liturgy. This structure has been in place since the earliest time in the Church. For a while we lost sight of this structure during the development of liturgy and the historical events that affected it. Sadly, the Liturgy of the Hours ceased to be the daily liturgy of most members of the Church when it became a liturgy prayed only by priests, monastics, and some religious men and women. Some of the sacraments were celebrated with only a Liturgy of the Sacrament. It is quite significant that with the revision of the rites of the Church after Vatican II, each celebration of the seven sacraments should now include a Liturgy of the Word. SC underscores the great importance of including sacred Scripture as a significant moment during liturgy, and remarks that the scriptural word discloses the meaning of the signs and actions (see nos. 24 and 51). In fact, SC goes so far as to say with respect to Mass that the Liturgy of the Word and the Liturgy of the Eucharist (and, by extension, the Liturgy of the Sacrament for the other seven sacraments) are related so closely that together they are a single act of worship (see no. 56). The *Catechism of the Catholic Church* (nos. 1153–1155) spells out how essential the Liturgy of the Word is in relation to the sign of the sacrament (that is, the Liturgy of the Sacrament). Word informs sign. The Liturgy of the Word helps us enter into a deeper meaning of the sacrament that is being celebrated. But even more, the close connection between word and sign unleashes each liturgical celebration as an enactment of the paschal mystery.

The rhythm between self-emptying and Life-receiving that marks the paschal mystery is the same rhythm that marks the dynamic between the Liturgy of the Word and the Liturgy of the Sacrament (in the Liturgy of the Hours, the rhythm unfolds between the psalmody and intercessions). In the unfolding of these two central parts of each sacrament, the proclamation of the Word (especially a Gospel) confronts us with a call to self-emptying, self-giving. We are challenged to hear God's Word and in that Word hear God's will for us. Even when the scriptural word we hear has a more affirmative context and is affirming and hope-filled, there is always a challenge to grow. Word confronts us in a very concrete way to examine who we are and how we are living our identity as members of the Body of Christ. Each celebration of the Liturgy of the Word ought to leave us a bit squirming, a bit uncomfortable. The summons and challenge we hear ought not to be ignored. When they come from wrestling with God's inspired Word, they convey an encounter with God's will for us. Sometimes the encounter is more gentle, sometimes it is more testing, sometimes it is more demanding. But always God's Word ought not be ignored.

We must not forget that the Liturgy of the Word is not all there is to our sacramental celebrations. The word carries us toward the sacramental sign. The dying is not all there is to the paschal mystery. The

Liturgy of the Sacrament calls us to enter into a moment of Life-receiving. This second major movement of the sacramental celebration encourages us to embrace the Life and strength God offers us in the sacrament. Our surrender enables a transformation of ourselves into being more perfect members of the Body of Christ.

Liturgy enacts the paschal mystery in its very ritual structure. And no matter where we are in our daily living, our celebration of liturgy carries us through both poles of the mystery, even when it is not so evident in our daily living. This is one reason why it is so important to celebrate liturgy often. It is one of the reasons why the celebration of Eucharist on Sunday (or Saturday evening) is the first precept of the Church (see CCC, 2042). But this is not a restrictive law; it is a freeing law. The precept is not just about taking away part of our Sunday to be in church. This law requiring us to celebrate the Eucharist every Sunday is essentially a law underscoring the necessity for us to have a ritual experience of the paschal mystery regularly, reminding us that this is who we are and how we are to live. Liturgy reinforces our clarity about how and why we are baptized into Christ's saving mystery. Our lives can be (and usually are) pretty messy. We can easily be bogged down in all the demands of taking up our cross each day (see Luke 9:23) that following Christ demands from us. Liturgy, even in our seeming darkest moments of life, carries us beyond the cross to resurrection. No wonder liturgy is the source (fount) and summit of the whole Christian life (see SC, 10)! Without liturgy we could easily lose sight of the exaltation that following Christ faithfully promises and that we live even now the gift of God's Life within us.

Liturgy as Source and Summit of Everyday Living

In language about the paschal mystery, we have been speaking of two poles; the language of Vatican II concerning liturgy speaks of two poles as well: source and summit. So we have two sets of two poles, and they are not mutually exclusive. Two parallels emerge: source||self-emptying and summit||Life-receiving.

By *source* of everyday living, of Gospel living, we are invited to think about liturgy as offering us all we need to deal in a good way with whatever life tosses at us. The liturgy is where we encounter God in the Triune Divine

Majesty. During liturgy we pray to the Father, through the Son, by the power of the Holy Spirit. More particularly, liturgy enacts the paschal mystery and in this continues in the here-and-now Jesus' saving mission. But more than this: as we participate fully, consciously, and actively in liturgy (see SC, 14) we share in and continue Jesus' saving mission.

Liturgical Participation

Sacrosanctum concilium most often speaks about "active participation" (for example, nos. 19, 27, 30, 41, 50, 113, 114, 121, 124). A close reading of these paragraphs makes clear that "active participation" includes responding and singing, postures and gestures, and other such external signs of joining in the liturgical celebration. We might think of "active participation" as our whole-body engagement with the liturgy. But this is not enough to enjoy the rich fruits liturgy offers. In addition to our bodies, our wills must be surrendered to the action of liturgy, which is nothing less than opening ourselves to allow God to transform us. We must consciously say yes to God and whatever God wills for us during this liturgy as well as during our daily living. Early on during liturgy we ought to utter something like "Take me and do with me what you will," and then mean it. This surrender can be quite challenging. Sometimes liturgy might urge us and our everyday living in a direction that we might not so willingly choose. Perhaps we are pressed to offer greater charity toward our neighbors, or to forgive the person who annoys us to distraction, or not to watch so much TV and rather to spend a bit more time in prayer, or to nourish others out of our abundance or graciously receive the nourishment others offer us, or to stand up to injustices. Conscious surrender to God's transformation during liturgy draws us toward self-emptying and self-giving. Conscious participation in liturgy consists of mindfully and willfully surrendering ourselves to the liturgical action.

It takes effort to participate actively—to be engaged whole-bodily during liturgy; conscious participation (a mindfully conscious surrender) pushes us to where we might not choose to go in living the Gospel and makes demands upon us. There is yet one more perspective on participation: full participation. This kind of participation includes whole-body and willful participation, but now takes us to the heart of the matter: We are to open ourselves spiritually to God's transformation of us into more perfect members of the Body of Christ. We must be open to receiving God's offer of new Life. Full participation is a total giving over of ourselves to be transformed by God into the Beloved he wishes us to be. Through this divine transforming action, we are constantly growing in our privilege of being Christ's Presence to all those we meet. Our openness to God's working in and through us goes beyond the ritual action itself. It enables us to be an instrument of Christ's saving mission. It draws us more deeply into the divine Life God offers us and helps us make our everyday choices out of an awareness of that Life. Full participation in liturgy moves us along our life journey with Christ toward the absolute fullness of Life that God offers us as we pass through our human death to eternal Life.

Liturgy as Source and Summit

Liturgy is the source of our identity as the risen Presence of Christ that we bring to our everyday living and to all we encounter. Liturgy is the source of the Life that strengthens us to accept the awesome task of continuing Christ's saving mission. Liturgy is the source of the Church's treasure of gifts of virtue, encouragement, and coming to full stature in Christ. "Full stature" takes us to the next pole of everyday liturgical living—that liturgy is the summit toward which all our everyday living is directed.

By *summit* of everyday living, of Gospel living, we are invited to think about liturgy as giving us a foretaste of who we are becoming: saints gathered around the eternal Presence of God in unending adoration. Liturgy, especially the Eucharistic banquet, is a foretaste of heaven (see SC no. 8). Liturgy as the summit of everyday living suggests that the choices we make each day of our lives are directed to where we are ultimately journeying: toward the fullness of Life in heaven. We are strengthened to make good choices—to do God's will—by the very Life of God that is given us. When we allow our everyday lives, bolstered by previous liturgical participation, to lead us back to liturgical celebration, we are completing a kind of circle: God gives us Life through the divine transformation that occurs during liturgy, and we come face to face during liturgy with the risen Christ, who calls us to a share in the fullness of his risen Life.

Something we Christians rarely think about or admit is that we are all called to holiness. It is telling that in *Lumen gentium* (LG), immediately after chapter 4 on the laity comes chapter 5 on "The Call to Holiness." Holiness is not something we receive at the end of a good life when we die so we can get to heaven. Holiness is God's gift of divine Life to us that we first receive at baptism and then deepen through sacraments and Gospel living every day of our lives. Holiness is not simply for those outstanding people the Church has formally recognized and calls saints. We are holy because Christ has joined us to him as members of his Body, the Church (see LG, 39). We are all saints. At liturgy we deepen this Life God offers us and grow toward its fullness. While celebrating liturgy we stand with all the angels and saints in praising God. Liturgy as the summit of everyday Christian living promises that God welcomes us into the divine embrace even as we are still firmly rooted here on earth. Liturgy gives us a little taste of heaven.

Fullness of Communion

Two other truths come to mind when we reflect on liturgy as the summit toward which all everyday Christian living moves. First, we do not journey to the fullness of Life by ourselves. Liturgy makes visible the Church, the Body of Christ. We need each other on this journey. Jesus promised that where two or three are gathered in his name, he is present (see Matthew 18:20). At liturgy, the whole Body of Christ is actually visible; at liturgy we are Church made visible. Not just Church as this limited gathering of members of the Body of Christ in this time and space, but the whole Church: past, present, and future members of the Body of Christ. We have traditionally called this the "communion of all saints." This large company of followers of Christ from all time is united as one. This is an incredible privilege. The communion of all saints stretches us beyond our own individual selves and links us in a particular way with each other. Communion is union with God and others.

> At liturgy, the whole Body of Christ is actually visible; at liturgy we are Church made visible.

Second, although holy Communion is one element in the Eucharistic rite, all liturgy enables a visible communion with God. God invites us to liturgy. God makes the divine Self present to us. God chooses to be present to us in this holy act. This visible communion with God and each other—in the very gathering together—is already a participation in the fullness of communion we will one day share with God and the saints in heaven. Liturgy as summit of our everyday living draws us beyond our limited time and space to participate in the unlimited time and space of divine Presence. While this visibility of communion is so obvious when we are actually gathered for liturgy, the communion with God and each other is not broken when we are dismissed from the ritual. Rather, the dismissal at the end of liturgy sends us forth to make visible to all the world what has been made visible to us in liturgy. We are the Body of Christ—the sacrament of Christ in the world—being sent forth to continue Jesus' saving mission.

Liturgy Sends Us on Mission

In one sense, liturgy is for our sake. It is for our own salvation. It is for us to grow in our relationship with God and each other. Liturgy benefits us when we participate actively, consciously, fully. But liturgy is not only for us. We have seen how liturgy transforms us. The transformation, nonetheless, is not just about us and our holiness. It is also about spending ourselves and all the goodness God bestows on us for others. Liturgy necessitates our reaching out to others to share the gifts God has bestowed on us. There is a circular movement here from God to us to others and, hopefully, back to God. There must be a movement from liturgy to mission, from mystery to ministry. Mystery points us to immersion in Christ; ministry points us to being Christ for others. Mystery without ministry turns us in on ourselves; ministry without mystery quickly collapses into activity for its own sake.

Mystery

Various New Testament letters (see especially St. Paul's Letter to the Colossians and the Letter to the Ephesians) develop a rich sense of mystery. Mystery can be understood as a threefold revelation of God's unfolding gift of salvation.

First, the broadest conception of mystery is that it is God's divine, secret plan of salvation from the beginning of time (see Colossians 1:26; Ephesians 3:9–10). From the creation of humankind, through the fall of Adam and Eve and the loss of the wonderful gifts that they enjoyed in the Garden of Eden, especially immortality, God never abandoned us. Through the original sin both death and evil entered into our existence. But God's tremendous mercy and love did not forsake us. God's secret plan was a relentless divine desire that we regain everything and more that was lost in the Garden. To this end God sent judges and kings and prophets to keep the covenantal relationship between the divine and the human before us. Time and time again we ignored God's overtures to entice us back to covenantal relationship with God. Here is the mystery: that God never gives up on us. No matter how obstinate, unhearing, unchanging we are at times, God keeps trying to draw us to the divine Self. The depths of the mystery of God's love can never be exhausted or fully comprehended. God will never forsake us (see, for example, the promise in Deuteronomy 31:6; this promise is repeated scores of times throughout sacred Scripture). The mystery of God's plan of salvation is that it can never be totally foiled. No matter how sinful humankind can be, no matter how often we do not listen to God's will being revealed in so many ways, no matter how much we try to go it alone, the mystery of God's plan still is an umbrella of divine mercy. God throughout all of history has gradually revealed the divine plan for our salvation. The most concrete and clear revelation of God's desire for our salvation, and how far God goes to fulfill that divine desire, takes place in the sending of the Divine Son to draw us more closely to his Father.

Second, then, another understanding of mystery is simply the Presence of the Person of Jesus Christ, who was sent to us on a redemptive mission (see, for example, Ephesians 3:11; Colossians 1:27). Jesus' whole life and ministry was directed to bringing us back to his Father, now in an even more intimate relationship. Through Jesus, we *see* his

Father (see, John 12:45 and 14:9). Jesus is the divine Presence sent to draw us into the mystery of God's salvation. He, the Second Person of the Holy Trinity, came to help us see more clearly and in a very specific way God's plan of salvation. Even when Jesus' ministry on earth was finished and he returned to his Father at the ascension, he did not leave us grasping for a path to realizing the mystery's glories. No, at the Last Supper when he commanded that we "do this in memory of me" (Luke 22:19), he was giving himself to us in perpetuity—but now even more intimately than when he walked this earth with his disciples while undertaking his saving mission. Now we receive his very Self-giving, his very Self as heavenly Food for our own journey of salvation. While the preeminent Self-giving of Jesus is the Eucharist Food and Drink, his Self-giving continues in each celebration of liturgy (sacraments and Liturgy of the Hours) and in any way we make ourselves open to his Presence.

Third, then, the mystery continues today in the celebration of liturgy, the enactment of the paschal mystery—that making present of God's divine plan of salvation in the very Person of Christ. All liturgy is an act of the risen Christ's Self-giving. But it is more than that. As we receive Christ in liturgy (in each of the sacraments and the Liturgy of the Hours in their own manner), we ourselves become instruments of God's divine plan. Immersing ourselves in the mystery and receiving God's unparalleled promise of Presence enables us to embrace the mission and ministry of the risen Christ. Ministry is an exercise of our baptismal priesthood, our share in Christ's high priesthood (see Hebrews 4:14—5:6 and 8:1–6; also CCC, 1546–1547). Ministry is essentially a mediation between God and God's people. The fruits of liturgy include a call to ministry.

Ministry

Ministry is both a call and a response. All ministry in the Church is ultimately a call from Jesus Christ to live out our baptismal commitment. Baptism makes us members of the Body of Christ, and as members of that Body we have a responsibility to help build it up to full stature in Christ (see Ephesians 4:13). Our response to that call during liturgy is self-giving that is directed to liturgy being celebrated in a meaningful, responsible, fruitful way for all.

When we think of ministries during liturgy, we tend to immediately think of specific, recognized liturgical ministries: presider, deacon, acolytes and servers, lectors, musicians, hospitality ministers, extraordinary ministers of holy Communion. Indeed, a typical Sunday Mass would necessitate a good number of people involved in these ministries. But it is telling how small a percentage of the registered members of a parish volunteer for these liturgical ministries. Often parishes have something like a "stewardship Sunday" (usually in the fall) when people are asked to project their monetary contributions to the parish (essential for making out a reasonable and balanced parish budget) as well as volunteer for various ministries, liturgical and otherwise. Some people tend to think it takes special talent to carry on these ministries (and some of them do require certain abilities), but they often forget or have never been taught that the most important liturgical ministry is the ministry of the assembly.

> Ministry is an exercise of our baptismal priesthood, our share in Christ high priesthood. Ministry is essentially a mediation between God and God's people. The fruits of liturgy include a call to ministry.

In other words, just by coming to liturgy those gathering are exercising their baptismal priesthood. Simply assembling is a ministry. Simply assembling is responding to the call to minister to the Body of Christ and participate in Jesus' saving mission. How so? The Body of Christ gathered together around Christ the Head (visible in the presence of the ordained presider) is a presence of the whole Church (see CCC, 1548–1549). Each one of us, in our surrender to being assembly, participates in the movement from being individual members of the Body to becoming the whole, visible Body. Our becoming the whole, visible Body of Christ is our response to the call to be one with Christ both as individuals and as a community.

A call is a very special invitation from God to participate in the unfolding events of salvation. If we consider some of the call narratives from the Old Testament (two well-known examples are the call of Moses in Exodus 3:1–5 and the call of Isaiah in Isaiah 6:1–3), we can detect certain elements that make up the call and response. First, there is a theophany—that is, a manifestation of divine Presence. The call is a call from God to service. In the case of Moses, the theophany came in the form of an angel who appears in the burning bush; in the case of Isaiah, the theophany came in a vision of God in the Temple. Second, there is an introductory word whereby God's Presence is made known—for example, the one called might be addressed by name. Third, a commission is given: what it is God wants the one being called to do. In the narrative of Moses's call, it was to go to Pharaoh and ask him to set the Israelites free. In the case of Isaiah, it was a call to be a prophet. Fourth, the one called tends to offer some objection as to why this is not a reasonable request by God. Sometimes the one called feels unworthy, sometimes the task is too great, sometimes the one called is simply not ready to leave a familiar life. But God is persistent in divine calls and does not like a no for an answer. Fifth, God always offers some reassurance that God will never leave the one called alone; God will always be with us. In some call narratives, a sixth element is a sign from God that the call is authentic.

When we consider all the people Scripture presents to us who answered a call from God, it is amazing that God doesn't always call the holiest people, the most intelligent people, or the most inspiring people. God calls those who come from different backgrounds and differing abilities. The issue is not our worthiness or our abilities, but that we respond with a yes to God's call and remain open to God's gifts to fulfill the call. Further, the call is not always dramatic, clear, once and for all, as in the case of St. Paul. Most often it is a quiet call in the depths of our hearts. God persists in the call unless we say no. But if we say no, we have missed an opportunity to serve others and grow in holiness.

Liturgy is the mystery; ministry is the mission. One call is to "passover" from mystery to ministry. Every liturgy, then, invites us to a paschal event. As we embrace that paschal event—the passing from mystery to ministry—we transform our everyday living into the same paschal event. Our surrender to the mystery joins our lives to the risen Christ's in whom we are and all that we do. Our everyday lives become an enactment of the paschal mystery. The paschal mystery is unleashed during liturgy in the ritual structure making present the rhythm of dying and rising, of self-emptying and Life-receiving. Moreover, this rhythm does not end with the conclusion of the liturgical event and the dismissal to mission. Our ritual leave-taking is a further unleashing of the paschal mystery into the ups and downs, the opportunities and boredom, the ordinariness and creativity of our everyday living. Everything we say and do each day can be a paschal event when we commit ourselves to Gospel living. Gospel living is liturgical living.

In the introduction, the question we posed to be addressed in this second chapter is, Why does liturgy enact the saving mystery of Christ in the here and now, in our very messy daily living? Liturgy enacts the saving mystery of Christ, first, through the structural rhythm of the ritual. Ritual is very concrete; it is at hand; we can analyze it, experience it, respond to it. Liturgy is external to us in that it invites us to internalize what is really happening. What is happening at liturgy is the enacting of the paschal mystery. Our everyday lives are surely concrete, but they are not as easily identifiable in terms of the unfolding of the paschal mystery. Our lives do not generally unfold in a measurable, predictable, clean, clear, and concrete ritual structure. Yes, for most of us most of the time, our lives tend to be messy. The wonder of it all is that God takes us where we are. God uses even the messiness of our lives to continue the divine Son's saving mystery. The transformation fashioned in us during liturgy is key: we are transformed into being more perfect members of the Body of Christ. That same transformation taking place during liturgy occurs when we are faithful to who we are—those baptized into Jesus' death and resurrection—and live accordingly. This is truly when liturgy is unleashed in all its power: when we are faithful to our baptismal commitment to be the Body of Christ, living as Jesus did. Liturgy nourishes us in this commitment. It reinforces our wills to make right choices in daily living. Our faithful yes to living the Gospel is paschal mystery living. Our faithful yes to living the Gospel shines forth from us as a liturgical spirituality.

> Liturgy is the mystery; ministry is the mission.

Chapter 2: To Review and Reflect

Liturgy makes present the rhythm of the paschal mystery.

- I participate most actively, consciously, and fully at liturgy when I . . .
- I experience liturgy as the source of the good I do during my daily Gospel living when . . .
- Liturgy is the summit of daily living and my whole life in that . . .

Liturgy as mystery urges us toward ministry as mission.

- I hear God's call most clearly as . . . to . . .
- The ministry I most urgently feel I need to embrace is . . .
- I experience the movement from mystery to ministry best when I . . .

From this chapter, I wish to remember . . .

3

LITURGICAL SPIRITUALITY UNCOVERED

Spirituality is a way of living. Spirituality is the converging of faith, values, commitments, morals, and choices we make each day, which are lived out as a seamless whole. The more specific the spirituality—for example, Benedictine spirituality—the more explicit are the requirements for being faithful to that spirituality. One could hardly be a vowed Benedictine religious or commit to being a Benedictine oblate without accepting a way of life as interpreted by St. Benedict and his rule. The dictum for Benedictines is *ora et labora*, prayer and work. The integration of prayer and work is characteristic of both Benedictine monastics and oblates. A Benedictine spirituality might be characterized as contemplation in action. Since all Benedictines are baptized, this particular spirituality is integrated into a more comprehensive and encompassing spirituality shared by all the baptized—namely, a liturgical spirituality. Liturgical spirituality is a way of living the rhythm of the paschal mystery, which we experience during liturgy. Liturgical spirituality mirrors in our daily living the mystery of liturgy. Liturgical spirituality is a way of living; it is characterized by liturgy being the focus of every aspect of our life. It is

> Liturgical spirituality is a way of living; it is characterized by liturgy being the focus of every aspect of our life.

the source and summit of our everyday Christian living (see SC, 10 and LG, 11). In this chapter we uncover further the rich meaning of liturgical spirituality and its implications for daily living.

The Call to Holiness

For all too many centuries various spiritualties have stressed humankind's fallen nature, our propensity to sin, and our unworthiness in the face of God's majesty. We much more readily consider ourselves sinners than saints. In fact, if we would ask our relatives and friends if they are saints, there would be great hesitation in answering at all and probably a great deal of discomfort as well. Someone once remarked after listening intently to a presentation on holiness that she had never heard before that she is holy; she only considered herself a sinner. How sad!

HOLINESS AND GRACE

Holiness is nothing less than being in the state of grace. However, we have for too long considered grace to be a quantity that we get: when we do something good, we get more grace; when we do something bad, we lose grace. The name of the game is to die with at least a drop of grace so that we at least go to purgatory. This concept of holiness and grace is deficient. Grace, in fact, is simply God's Life dwelling within us through the power of the Holy Spirit. Grace establishes a relationship of mutual love and friendship. We first receive divine Life at baptism, and our daily journey with Christ is about deepening the graced relationship we have with God. A key word here is *relationship*. Holiness is a state of being in relationship with God. Grace, God's Life, is what enables this divine-human relationship. We protect this relationship, we grow in this relationship, we thrive in this relationship. There is much we ourselves contribute to this relationship. However, grace is always a divine gift. Grace is the *power* of the Holy Spirit acting within us to transform us. Grace is our participation in divine Life. We do not *earn* the grace of relationship. We live in such a way as to be faithful to the Life that God offers.

Grace is a free gift of God to which we respond in faith and love. Grace is a mystery we can only know by eyes of faith. We cannot see grace; but we can see the effects of grace, which is a life lived in conformity to

Christ, a Gospel way of living. Further, grace establishes a tapestry of relationships with God, self, others, and creation. We are not holy in isolation, but in relation to all who are and all that is. Being holy—living a graced life—is visible in the way we choose to relate to everything around us. In general, grace is God's loving concern, a concern so wonderful that God chooses to dwell within us. Grace also is the basis for all the blessings God gives, for all God's wonderful gifts. We experience God's gift of grace in the beauty of each person, the beauty of creation, and the beauty of our own selves as we grow in our relationship with God and others. Holiness is a gift that elicits a thankful response, not simply in words, but in the manner of living we choose.

Grace is God's favor, a free and undeserved help for our response to the divine call to become children of God, adopted daughters and sons of God, partakers of the divine nature, inheritors of eternal Life. In other words, grace is the gift of our baptism to be the beloved of God. Because holiness is a gift of God, not something we earn as a reward for doing something good, we can speak of a call to holiness.

Holiness and God's call

The call to holiness is a call to share in God's triune inner Life; it is a call to be faithful in our daily living of the Life that God has given us. Holiness is accepting and living grace as God's self-communication, and through us God is manifested to the world. The call to holiness is a lifelong response from each of us to live the love, care, compassion, forgiveness, hope, and promise that God has revealed throughout the ages.

God's call to holiness certainly comes in a unique way through the risen Christ who invites us to share in his saving mission. Nonetheless, God's call to holiness has been sent forth from the very beginning of creation. After their fall, Adam and Eve hid from God when they heard God stirring in the Garden of Eden. God called to them, inquiring where they were (see Genesis 3:8–9). God pursued Adam and Eve; sin caused them to hide from God. The unique, intimate relationship with God that Adam and Eve enjoyed before the fall changed. Now they would toil for their needs rather than have them abundantly and freely given by God (see Genesis 3:17–19). Nevertheless, despite the disruption of the pristine divine-human relationship at the beginning of creation, God has never ceased to call us to holiness. God has never not made known the divine desire to be in intimate relationship with us.

Holiness is such a centerpiece of the divine-human relationship that Leviticus, the "law book" of the Old Testament, addresses the issue of holiness to a great extent. Chapters 17 to 26 are typically called by Scripture scholars the "holiness code." In these chapters is the oft-repeated "law" to be holy as God is holy (see, for example, Leviticus 11:44–45). What a lofty command! Our immediate instinct is that to be holy as God is holy is not possible. After all, we are human, we sin, and we disrupt relationships rather all too easily. Yes, the command is there and is repeated. Holiness is of the essence of who God is; we are holy because we are gifted by God with a share in divine Life. We do not deserve holiness; God calls us to holiness simply because God is the greatest Lover there ever has been. Holiness is a sign that we are the beloved of our Creator. God calls all of his beloved to be holy: "Be holy, for I, the LORD your God, am holy" (Leviticus 19:2a).

> We do not deserve holiness; God calls us to holiness simply because God is the greatest Lover there ever has been.

We who are the Body of Christ are holy (see Romans 12:1). We who are baptized are God's chosen ones (see Colossians 3:12, 15), God's holy ones, God's saints. It is noteworthy how many of St. Paul's letters greet the Christians to whom he is writing by addressing them as those called to be holy, called to be saints (see, for example, Romans 1:7; 1 Corinthians 1:2; 2 Corinthians 1:1; Philippians 1:1). This call to be holy lies at the very foundation of our living a liturgical spirituality. Liturgy is the fount of holiness. If we choose to live the Gospel, we must drink deeply of that fount. Liturgy is the visible acting out of our answer to God's call to holiness. Liturgy transforms our very being—who we are—so that all our doing—continuing Jesus' saving mission—is authentic and fruitful. Liturgical spirituality is expressed in both being and doing.

The Being and Doing of Liturgical Spirituality

Living a liturgical spirituality is not only a privilege, but also a response to a call. The call is from God to all who are members of the Body of Christ. The call is to beings who respond with doing. The being is the graced beloved of God that we are, and the doing is taking up the responsibility of ministry, which is nothing less that carrying forth in the here and now the saving ministry of the risen Christ. Like liturgical spirituality itself, ministry is first a matter of being, then a matter of doing. All we do for Christ and his Church must flow from who we are. If our identity as the Presence of Christ is not at the basis of whatever we do in ministry, then all we are doing is getting a job done. When we work out of who we are, which is to say when we work out of a liturgical spirituality, then every moment of every day is a worthwhile ministry.

Being

The *being* of liturgical spirituality is nothing less than living our baptismal identity. We are the Body of Christ immersed in paschal mystery's rhythm of dying and rising, self-emptying and Life-receiving. We are a living sacrifice united with Christ our Head. Because we share the same common identity in Christ, our being expresses a new way of being together in community. We no longer live for ourselves or for just those close to us, but we live for all others. No one is beyond our sphere of loving and caring. We are sisters and brothers in Christ, a family of humanity. Ministry flows from our being quite naturally because as we grow more aware in our daily living of our whole being—of who we are, of our identity in Christ—and as our desire to live the Gospel as Jesus did increases, then like Jesus we naturally and graciously reach out to anyone who crosses our path. Ministry is not limited to specific works or actions; ministry is first and foremost an expression of our fidelity to who we are and were created to be. Ministry is a matter of being the risen Presence of Christ for others. Being the Presence of Christ must be our Christian way of living. This is communicating the liturgical spirituality to which we commit ourselves when we consciously live out our baptismal identity.

Doing as Ministry

At times, nevertheless, we do take up a specific ministry, a specific way of serving others. This may be a salaried staff position such as deacon, pastoral associate, religious educator, teacher in a Catholic school, or perhaps a liturgical ministry such as lector or extraordinary minister of holy Communion. Or there are service ministries such as altar server, sacristan, hospitality ministers of various kinds, individuals who take care of the seasonal environments, janitors, and many others. In each of these ministries and others not mentioned here, the minister is sharing a unique gift to build up the Body of Christ that is given by the Holy Spirit. During years of lived experience as members of the Body of Christ, we discern the unique gift we have been given to serve others in the Church.

The creative tension that describes the paschal mystery and liturgical spirituality reflects the demands of ministry and the joy of being in Christ. This creative tension is played out in both liturgy, where we experience the rhythm in the very structure of the ritual, and in everyday life, where we experience the tension in the normal flow of daily living (especially when we take time to reflect on our life and how it unfolds each day). Liturgical celebration takes us beyond the ritual moment to everyday living, and in this rhythm between liturgy and life we are compelled toward living a spirituality which includes taking up a ministerial task. Ministry is not just the call of a few. All of us who participate in liturgy are called to fulfill some ministry, some work that visibly builds up the Church, the Body of Christ. The call to ministry may well be to give oneself over to one of the Church's established ministries in pastoral work, education, or liturgical ministry. But it may also well be discovering the unique ways in other aspects of our lives—family, work, leisure—that we can witness to Christ's risen Presence and call others to good lives simply by the way we live the Gospel.

At times we might be more conscious of our ministry flowing from our liturgical spirituality. We might be more conscious of the rhythm of the paschal mystery unfolding in our lives. Perhaps we are being especially challenged to be faithful to the Gospel; our good choices in the face of the difficulty help us be very aware of our being members of the Body of Christ. At other times, the demands of fulfilling a ministry might outshine our sense of being. When we take those precious, quiet times for reflection on how and Who we are living, the seeming imbalance between being and doing can come into focus. It is not possible to be conscious of everything about ourselves all the time. Our focus shifts between being and doing at differing times of the day, week, year. Our lives flow in a rhythm—in fact, in many kinds of rhythms. And so it is with liturgical spirituality. Liturgy helps us become familiar with the many rhythms we incorporate in our daily being and doing.

Daily, Weekly, Yearly Rhythm of Liturgical Spirituality

The rhythm characteristic of liturgy and, therefore, of liturgical spirituality is the rhythm that exemplifies the paschal mystery. The very word *paschal* suggests the rhythm as a "passing": From death to risen Life, from self-emptying to Life-receiving, from self-giving surrender to fullness of Life. This rhythm occurs in our daily living, but distractions, coinciding events, regular demands on our time tend to conceal it. On the other hand, this rhythm unfolds structurally in every liturgy and is at hand through our senses: It is observable, able to be recognized and experienced in the here and now. An analysis of the structure of liturgical celebrations makes the paschal mystery apparent as a daily, weekly, yearly rhythm of living.

Daily Rhythm

Throughout the Judeo-Christian Tradition, daily prayer has been the norm. St. Paul admonishes the Christians at Thessolonika to pray without ceasing (see 1 Thessalonians 5:17); that is, Christians are to be oriented to God at all times, even outside of formal prayer times. Still, it seems second nature for believers to pray at rising in the morning, a time to thank God for a new day and pray for our needs, and at retiring at night, a time to seek forgiveness for the faults of the day and thank God for the many blessings that have come our way. The psalms are prayers that were on the lips of faithful Jews throughout their day. There is ample evidence in the Acts of the Apostles—that inspired Scripture text getting us in touch with how the early Christian communities received and lived the paschal mystery—that Christians, like our Jewish sisters and brothers, prayed at the third (about mid-morning), sixth (at noon), and ninth (about mid-afternoon) hours (see, for example, Acts 2:46; 3:1; 10:9; 10:30).

Many of us grew up praying at morning and evening and at other times of the day. The "Angel of God, My Guardian Dear" prayer was most likely the first morning prayer many of us learned. Catholic school children sometimes prayed together the "Morning Offering" before the school day began. We learned as small children to pray before and after meals (roughly coinciding with the third, sixth, and ninth hours). We prayed before going to bed, and when we were a bit older we were probably taught how to examine our consciences. All this is well and good, and certainly helped many people grow in holiness. But these were devotional, private prayers. Other than perhaps daily Mass, the laity did not pray liturgically every day. This was not true in the early Church.

In the early Church, the baptized would gather in a community at both morning and evening for prayer. By the fourth century, with the peace of Constantine, the prayer began to take on a more universal and fixed structure consisting mainly of praying psalms and intercessions. As time went on and the Christian community grew in numbers and size, the prayer was even more formalized with various liturgical elements being added to the ritual structure. Eventually the daily prayer of the Church—to accommodate the spiritual needs of monastics—expanded to more times (hours) of the day for prayer, to a more complex structure, and to more demands in praying it since it was largely a sung prayer. Around the sixth century, this communal prayer ceased being the daily prayer of the whole Church and became the prayer largely of monastics, clergy, and the women and men religious required to pray it by their constitutions. For the most part deprived of daily liturgical prayer, naturally the laity reverted to devotional prayer that suited their spirituality. It was not until *Sacrosanctum concilium* was promulgated in 1963 that the laity were once again encouraged to take part in the Church's traditional daily liturgical prayer (see SC, 100), now known as the Liturgy of the Hours. It has taken these past six decades since the council for the Liturgy of the Hours to be accessible for the laity and understood as their baptismal right and privilege. The Liturgy of the Hours is the prayer of all the baptized. Several publishers now include in their hymnals or daily prayer magazines a simple and manageable morning and evening prayer that follows the ancient structure of psalmody and intercessions. This format makes it easy and accessible for even busy laity. It frames their day in Morning and Evening Prayer and its rhythm of paschal mystery.

Both the time and structure of the Church's daily prayer embody a paschal mystery rhythm. Let us begin with time and consider first the two "hinge" prayers (see SC, 89a) of Morning Prayer and Evening Prayer. Each day begins with sunrise and ends with sunset, even if there is a thick cloud cover and we cannot see the sunshine. This rhythm happens: morning/evening, sunup/sundown. In the framework of a paschal mystery rhythm, this daily cosmic event plays on words in English: as the sun rises, we celebrate the Son rising. We begin each day, then, by immersing ourselves in the new Life of the resurrection. At the end of the day, we experience darkness coming on as the sun sets (dies) and so we celebrate the Son's dying. We end each day, then, by immersing ourselves in the mystery of Jesus' death on the cross for our salvation. What a beautiful gift! Each day we are invited to remember, to celebrate, to make present liturgically Jesus' death and resurrection when we join with other members of the Body of Christ throughout the world in praying the Church's Morning and Evening Prayer. Each day of our lives unfolds within the rhythm of sunup and sundown, with a rhythm of rising and dying. Praying the Church's daily liturgy of Morning and Evening Prayer frames our whole day in the saving mystery of Christ. We begin and end our day with a prayer bringing to our consciousness who we are as baptized members of the Church plunged into Christ's saving mystery.

Beyond the paschal mystery time frame of daily liturgical prayer, the very structure of Morning and Evening Prayer plunges us into the paschal mystery. The *General Instruction of the Liturgy of the Hours* describes the Liturgy of the Hours as praise and supplication (see no. 2). Here is where we can detect the paschal mystery rhythm becoming apparent in the structure of the prayer.

God's praise is sung (literally or figuratively) in the psalms assigned to each day. One might question how we can claim the psalms are praise when so many of them—well over half the psalms, in fact—are laments; so many of the psalms decry our miserable human condition. But even the laments, as their verses progress, are praise. These psalms begin with an address of God, then move to the lament, the complaint or the dismay over the human condition, but the laments do not wallow in the grievance. No, the psalmist is moved to praise and thankfulness as God's wonderful deeds are remembered on our behalf; the psalmist remembers God's fidelity in face of our infidelity and remembers Gods' trustworthy mercy and compassion.

Other psalms have as their theme praise, thanksgiving, petition for forgiveness, and other such prayer sentiments. How we pray the psalms has much to do with whether we experience them as Life-giving. It is helpful to remember that the psalms are poetic songs. Ideally, they are meant to be sung. This, however, is not always possible. So, if not singing the psalms, whether alone or in a group, a good practice is to recite/pray the psalms aloud slowly in such a way that the poetic rhythm of each psalm is felt deep within ourselves. True, this takes some practice. Feeling the rhythm of the psalms is already our entering into the paschal mystery rhythm that Morning and Evening Prayer embody. Psalmody as the first major structural part of Morning and Evening Prayer opens us to God's Presence and offer of new Life. It is a Life-receiving moment of joyful praise.

The Life promised in the psalms is balanced by the next major structural part, which is intercessory prayer. Confident of God's Presence and offer of new Life, we are emboldened to make known our petitions. In so many ways each of us is poor and needy. Liturgical intercessions, while they may include very personal and specific prayers, are to be primarily general intercessions praying for the needs of the whole Body of Christ and the world. Praying this daily liturgy is an exercise of our baptismal priesthood whereby, in naming our needs, in recognizing our dependence on God, in owning our own weaknesses and failures, we are compelled to surrender ourselves to God's care and goodness. In intercessory prayer we recognize that we are still on the journey toward fuller Life. Intercessory prayer reminds us that all is not well with ourselves and our world. Much more needs to happen before the wholeness and well-being of salvation is realized for all. Intercessory prayer calls us to die to ourselves, to surrender ourselves to Gospel living without counting the cost. Intercessory prayer is the dying moment of the daily paschal mystery rhythm.

> Intercessory prayer reminds us that all is not well with ourselves and our world. Intercessory prayer calls us to die to ourselves, to surrender ourselves to Gospel living without counting the cost. Intercessory prayer is the dying moment of the daily paschal mystery rhythm.

Both the time of the Church's daily prayer that occurs at morning and evening, and the structure of the daily prayer that is essentially a prayer of praise and petition, capture a paschal mystery rhythm. When we are faithful to this prayer, we are reminded each day upon rising in the morning and upon retiring at night that our whole day in between must be marked by this saving rhythm. The daily liturgy of the Church helps us remember the rhythm of dying and rising; this is the foundation of liturgical spirituality. The daily liturgy of the Church reminds us of how we allow our days to unfold as being and doing in the name of the risen Christ.

Weekly Rhythm

We have already pointed to *Sacrosanctum concilium*'s insistence that liturgy is the fount and summit of the whole Christian life (see SC, 10). We noted that *Lumen gentium* narrows down the source and summit of the whole Christian life to the Eucharistic sacrifice (see LG, 11). If it is true that the celebration of Mass is the source and summit of our living (and it is!), then it makes sense to say that there is also a weekly rhythm to our living the paschal mystery, unfolding between the six weekdays largely given to various works, and Sunday largely given to resting in God's largesse. So much needs to be said about Sunday, especially since in our society Sunday has largely lost its meaning as a celebration of resurrection, a day of rest, and the day to strengthen our relationship with God and loved ones.

It was on the first day of the week, Sunday, that all four Gospels tell us Jesus arose from the dead (see Matthew 28:1; Mark 16:2; Luke 24:1; John 20:1). Sunday, from the very beginning of the Church, has been associated with remembering Jesus' resurrection, especially by the Breaking of the Bread—one early name for the Mass. The *Catechism of the Catholic Church* makes two especially poignant statements about why Sunday is the centerpiece of our week. First, when we gather on Sunday we gather as a community for a very specific purpose:

> Participation in the communal celebration of the Sunday Eucharist is a testimony of belonging and of being faithful to Christ and to his Church. The faithful give witness by this to their communion in faith and charity. Together they testify to God's holiness and their hope of salvation. They strengthen one another under the guidance of the Holy Spirit. (CCC, 2182)

Without gathering, we cannot be a visible community witnessing to where we belong: together in Christ. Our Sunday gathering is an expression of our baptismal identity, unity, and our ongoing yes to continuing Jesus' saving ministry. We strengthen and encourage each other in the work of salvation in our being together, and particularly because at Mass we call down the Holy Spirit upon us to make us one in Christ.

Second, we gather on Sunday in order to celebrate Jesus' resurrection: "The Church celebrates the day of Christ's Resurrection on the 'eighth day,' Sunday, which is rightly called the Lord's Day (cf. SC, 106)" (CCC, 2191). Eighth Day? But we only have seven days in a week! The name for Sunday in the early Church was the "Lord's Day" or the "Eighth Day." Sunday is a day out of time, which is the reason for Sunday being a day of rest recalling our eternal rest with God in heaven. Calling Sunday the Eight Day reminds us that Sunday is eschatological time—that is, a time when we celebrate the fullness of Life that is to come when we enter into our eternal glory. Sunday as the "Eighth Day" reminds us that at the Eucharistic celebration we unite ourselves with all the saints in heaven, praising God for the great work of salvation (see SC, 8). Sunday is a day to celebrate glory—God's glory and our own participation in it.

Celebration here is not simply exuberance or unmitigated joy—hoopla. Liturgical *celebration* has a much deeper meaning. Liturgy's celebration is intimately connected with the free time that interrupts work. Here is the weekly rhythm: we work six days of the week as if everything depends on us and our efforts; we rest on the first day of the week as if everything depends on God (which it ultimately does). True liturgical celebration is Sunday time free from daily work time. Sunday is a special time for us to renew ourselves; to remember God's goodness to us; to dare to be different in how we pray, eat, come together as Christian community and as family. Sunday is a special time because every Sunday we celebrate Easter. Obviously, each Sunday may be less exuberantly festive than Easter Sunday itself, but this doesn't take away the beauty and joy of each Sunday as a celebration of Easter, of resurrection.

Further, if each Sunday is a celebration of Easter, then each Friday is a day to remember the cross. Friday remains a day for fasting and penance, even if we are no longer obliged to abstain from meat on Fridays

> ESCHATOLOGY COMES FROM THE GREEK WORD **ESCHATON**, MEANING "LAST." IT IS AN AREA OF THEOLOGY CONCERNED WITH THE COMING OF CHRIST ON THE "LAST DAY." ESCHATOLOGY EXPLORES DEATH, JUDGMENT, RESURRECTION OF THE BODY, HEAVEN, PURGATORY, AND HELL.

(except, in the United States, during Lent and on Ash Wednesday). Our fasting and penance on Fridays is directly connected with the feasting on Sundays. Our hunger—experienced both physically and spiritually—on Friday readies us to approach the Eucharistic Banquet Table on Sundays and eat and drink the only nourishment that can truly satisfy us: the Body and Blood of the risen Christ. Friday to Sunday directs our attention each week to the paschal mystery, the death and resurrection of Jesus.

The Eucharistic celebration in its very structure enacts—makes present—a rhythm between the two poles of the paschal mystery, between dying and rising, between self-emptying and Life-receiving. The depth of the mystery of the Eucharistic celebration is the continual Self-giving of the risen Christ to us as Word and Sacrament. Eucharist calls us to respond to the risen Christ's Self-giving with our own surrender to the ritual action. In the Liturgy of the Word, God's living Word is proclaimed to us, the Word that points the way to salvation. Particularly in the Gospels, where the inspired evangelists and the Church have preserved for us insight into Jesus' life, ministry, death, resurrection, and ascension, are we challenged to die to self and live as Christ showed us how to live. We hear proclaimed week after week how Jesus ministered to others by teaching and preaching, healing and forgiving, caring and loving. The Liturgy of the Word invites us to the self-giving (dying to self) that Jesus still makes present.

Each week we are dismissed from the Eucharistic celebration to live what has been proclaimed. Each week we are reminded that daily we must take up our cross, deny ourselves (see Luke 9:23), die to ourselves for our own salvation and that of others. The Eucharistic rite opens us to this daily task of dying to self at the universal prayer (prayer of the faithful) when we pray for the Church, for the salvation of the world, for those in any need, and for ourselves (see GIRM, 70). Simply praying these intercessions is a stimulus to cooperate with God in making happen that for which we pray. Our intercessions lay out a manner of relating to others and the world. Praying the intercessions is already an invitation to die to ourselves for the sake of others. The entire Liturgy of the Word urges us to enter into the dying pole of the paschal mystery.

If this were all there were to the Eucharistic celebration, we could get discouraged quite quickly. All this demand about dying to ourselves seems not very encouraging. But the Church and the development of the

Eucharistic ritual over the last two millennia never leave us simply with the dying pole of the paschal mystery. The Liturgy of the Word opens onto the Liturgy of the Eucharist. In this second major division of the Eucharistic celebration, we are invited to place ourselves on the altar along with the bread and wine to be transformed by the action of the Holy Spirit; we pray and remember the risen Christ's life and Self-giving for us in the Eucharistic Prayer; we process to the Messianic Banquet table and receive the Body and Blood of the risen Christ. St. Augustine rhapsodizes on what happens when we take and eat at the Eucharistic Banquet, in a well-known sermon from the fifth century:

> If you are to understand what it means to be the Body of Christ,
> hear what Paul has to say:
> "Now you are the Body of Christ and individually members of it" (1 Cor 12:27).
> If you are the Body of Christ and members of it,
> then it is that mystery which is placed on the Lord's table:
> you receive the mystery,
> which is to say the Body of Christ,
> your very self.
> You answer Amen to who you are
> and in the answer you embrace yourself.
> You hear Body of Christ and answer Amen.
> Be a member of Christ's Body,
> that your Amen be true.
> (St. Augustine, Sermon 272; translation by author)

Such beautiful and challenging words! St. Augustine is quite clear about our being placed on the Eucharistic table, that we receive the very Body of Christ, that we become more perfectly that Body. Our amen to the mystery is to be true; it is true when we take up the challenge of liturgical spirituality. However, before we take up even more explicitly the challenge of liturgical spirituality, we have one more rhythm to delve into.

Yearly rhythm

We have uncovered a daily rhythm of liturgical spirituality—that of daily prayer which unfolds the paschal mystery between Morning Prayer and Evening Prayer, between sun/Son rising and sun/Son dying. We have also attended to a weekly rhythm of the paschal mystery between the challenges of weekday dying to self to live the Gospel and the Life-giving Sunday rest celebrating the resurrection. Each of these two rhythms has a liturgical structure wherein lies the paschal mystery. As we now turn to a yearly rhythm of liturgical spirituality, we have no specific liturgical structure to examine. The yearly rhythm, nevertheless, does have a liturgical document to guide our reflection, the *Lectionary for Mass*, which contains the cycle of Scripture readings for each day and season. The schema or organization of readings throughout the year is certainly not haphazard. The internal logic of the lectionary immerses us in a yearly celebration of the saving mystery of Christ. Herein lies our rhythm of the paschal mystery.

The liturgical year is divided into several "seasons" or thematic groupings of Sundays and weeks that do not evenly divide the days, weeks, and months. The season with the largest number of Sundays and weeks is Ordinary Time, which is divided into two parts. There are up to thirty-four weeks in Ordinary Time, which is about 65 percent of the whole year. We might group the rest of the year into "festal time." Advent and Lent are preparatory weeks for the two great festivals of Christmas and Easter, those celebrations that immerse us in two key events of Jesus' life and ministry. So we have two large groupings; let us look at how these help us immerse ourselves in a yearly rhythm of liturgical spirituality, a rhythm of living the paschal mystery.

Ordinary Time is really poorly named because this time of the year is truly extraordinary in terms of Gospel living. The Latin title for this time of the year is *tempus per annum*, translated as "time through the year." Makes good sense to us; this is what is chronologically happening. So from where does *ordinary* time come? We count the Sundays/weeks of this liturgical season using ordinal numbers (*ordinalis* in Latin), hence second, third, fourth Sunday/week in Ordinary Time and so on up to the thirty-fourth or last Sunday in Ordinary Time, which is also called the Solemnity of Our Lord Jesus Christ the King of the Universe.

Ordinary Time is counting time, but certainly not ordinary. What characterizes this liturgical season is a fairly sequential reading of one of the three Synoptic Gospels: Matthew, Mark, or Luke. Thus, the lectionary is divided into a three-year cycle of readings for the Sunday Eucharistic celebration, simply named "Year A" (Matthew's Gospel is proclaimed), "Year B" (the year of Mark's Gospel), and "Year C" (when we journey through Luke's Gospel). Omitting those Gospel pericopes (selections) that pertain to the festal seasons, Ordinary Time begins with the initial works of Jesus' public ministry, recorded after the story of the incarnation, which is proclaimed during the Christmas season. As Ordinary Time begins, we hear about the call of the first disciples, Jesus' first miracles, and his early preaching. During this first part of Ordinary Time, which occurs between the Christmas Season and the beginning of Lent, we ourselves are to hear anew and surrender to Jesus' call. We are to walk once again with Jesus and his disciples on his journey to Jerusalem, a journey to the cross and resurrection. What is rightly extraordinary about Ordinary Time is that we are privileged to walk with Jesus through a Gospel, entering into Jesus' very life and ministry.

We might say that Ordinary Time is the teaching time of the liturgical year. As we hear a Synoptic Gospel proclaimed chapter after chapter, Sunday after Sunday, we hear a blueprint for our own everyday Gospel living. It is as though we were in that company of first disciples who listened and learned from Jesus his way of life.

The second part of Ordinary Time occurs from the Monday after Pentecost until Saturday after the thirty-fourth and last Sunday in Ordinary Time (Christ the King). There is a beautiful movement in our Ordinary Time journey as we walk with Jesus and learn how to live the Gospel from his very words. We begin Ordinary Time with a call to discipleship and end with a vision of the glory to which our journey takes us—to be eternally with Christ the King, sharing in his fullness of Life. Ordinary Time asks us to surrender ourselves daily (die to ourselves) so that we might faithfully reach the end of our Christian journey. Ordinary Time is the dying pole of the paschal mystery. We learn how we must die to ourselves in order to be faithful followers of the risen Christ living as he did.

Although Ordinary Time is the longest liturgical season, we do have the rest of the year to consider. Ordinary Time is counterbalanced by the festal seasons. Ordinary Time focuses on the whole mystery of Jesus

Christ. The festal seasons focus on two specific events: the incarnation and the resurrection. Each of these events is so important that the seasons of Christmas and Easter have preparatory seasons, Advent and Lent, respectively. The festal seasons are not mutually exclusive, nor ought we to consider them in historical terms such as Jesus needs to be born before he can die and rise. No, something much more sublime is being presented during these weeks of the year.

Christmas and Easter are two sides of the same saving mystery. Christmas is about far more than the birth of a baby, even of the divine Son. The Second Person of the Holy Trinity emptied himself of being God (see Philippians 2:6–7). Let's think about that: emptied himself of who he is as a divine Being? Why would the Second Person of God do that? Because God loves us infinitely, because God chooses to save us, because God desires an even more intimate relationship with us than was given us at creation, which is that we are created in the image of God (see Genesis 1:27). By Jesus' emptying himself of divinity and taking on our nature, our humanity, God invites us to enter a whole new relationship with the divine. Jesus' taking on human flesh and becoming like us in all things except sin opened the way for us to receiving the divine Life that God offers us. The collect for the Mass during the Day on Christmas eloquently states the mystery of the incarnation. This collect petitions that "we may share in the divinity of Christ, / who humbled himself to share in our humanity" (RM). Can our prayer be any clearer about our deepest desire as those baptized into Christ?

Christmas makes known the divine-human exchange that the incarnation makes possible. Easter makes known the same wondrous exchange in that Jesus' resurrection from the dead destroyed death and includes a promise that those of us faithful to Jesus' way of life, faithful to Gospel living, will also share in this risen Life. The festal seasons are about our share in divine Life. The festal seasons are the Life-receiving pole of the paschal mystery unfolding in our yearly liturgical celebrations.

The paschal mystery is at hand in the rhythm between Ordinary Time and festal time. As we journey through each liturgical year we are summoned to die to self and receive the new Life God offers us. This yearly journey into

> As we journey through each liturgical year we are summoned to die to self and receive the new Life God offers us.

the saving mystery of Christ challenges us to choose Jesus' life as a way of living. This yearly journey challenges us to grasp liturgical spirituality as our response to the call to walk with Jesus daily, weekly, yearly through death to new Life.

The Challenge of Liturgical Spirituality

We face many challenges as we incorporate liturgical spirituality into a way of living, which is nothing less than our daily participation in the work of salvation. Since the rhythm of Christian living is embedded in liturgical prayer, the most pervasive challenge of liturgical spirituality is to begin to see the paschal mystery rhythm in both liturgy and daily living.

The first challenge of liturgical spirituality is to get to know the risen Christ intimately. We cannot encounter his life in liturgy and live it in our daily comings and goings if we do not really know who he is and what he desires for us. While liturgy is certainly one way to encounter Christ and come to know him personally, we must guard against taking liturgy for granted. Nothing magic happens during liturgy. Celebrating liturgy well takes effort: On our part as individuals, and on the whole assembly as the Body of Christ.

Further, a good and transforming celebration of liturgy takes serious preparation. This means that most of us will probably need to take a good look at our priorities and arrange our schedules to include some quality prayer time as well as set time aside to engage with, for example, the Mass texts before we come to the Sunday celebration. We would need to establish a rhythm of daily Morning and Evening Prayer and be faithful to it so that this beautiful daily liturgy becomes a lifelong habit of prayer framing our day in the paschal mystery. If we don't pray each day, if we aren't attuned to Christ's Presence to us, if we don't make an effort to get to know Christ personally, and if we don't liturgically enter into the dying and rising rhythm of the paschal mystery, then it will be challenging to come to liturgy and encounter Christ. Liturgical spirituality is most aptly nourished and strengthened by the celebration of liturgy itself.

Choosing to make liturgical spirituality a way of living can be a daunting task, but many resources are now available to help us meet this challenge. Daily lectionary readings for Mass can be downloaded to smart phones; they can be found on various websites; daily prayer magazines with both a simple daily Morning and Evening Prayer as well as the Mass texts are also available for a modest subscription price. With resources readily at hand, it is much easier to enter into the rhythm of liturgical prayer, which bolsters a liturgical spirituality. We do not need to reinvent the proverbial wheel each day for our prayer life. All we need to do is try some of the resources that are available and see which ones help us the most.

Another challenge of living from liturgy is to consider it a baptismal privilege rather than a burden. If we see liturgical spirituality as a burden in our daily routine—one more thing we need to "get in"—then it is difficult for this spirituality to become part of who we are and how we live each day; it is hard for it to become a habit of who we are. This is a transition from task to welcome joy, from doing to being. When our daily, weekly, and yearly liturgical prayer becomes so much a part of us that we miss it, we long for it, we hunger for it, when something gets in the way of liturgy (for example, a sick child's needs or an unexpected phone call from someone asking for help), then we know we are well on the way to making liturgical spirituality the center of our lives, truly a part of us describing who we are.

One more challenge: We must be gentle with ourselves as we grow into the rhythm of the paschal mystery. Sometimes an opportunity to give of oneself is presented, and for some reason we miss it. Or at other times it might seem that we are only giving and do not experience the Life-receiving that is the other pole of the paschal mystery. We have said that life is messy; we are not always aware of the rhythm we are trying to live. This is when liturgy can be such a tremendous comfort, for no matter what our disposition at liturgy, the paschal mystery is enacted there. God is patient with us as we learn how to pattern our lives on that of the divine Son. We must be patient with ourselves in our learning and growing process.

In the introduction, the question we posed to be addressed in this third chapter is, Why does choosing to make liturgical spirituality the center of our lives affect who we are and what we do? The simple answer to this question is that liturgical spirituality is a way of living our baptismal identity and commitment. We are members of the Body of Christ. To be faithful to this identity we must learn who Christ is, how he lived, and how it is possible to continue his saving ministry in our here-and-now reality. Our choice to do this or that good becomes easier as we grow in our self-knowledge as members of the Body of Christ. While we can learn intellectually about liturgical spirituality, it is truly uncovered in our celebrating and living it. Liturgical spirituality is a matter of putting on Christ (see, for example, Romans 13:14) so that we can say with St. Paul that we don't live by ourselves, but Christ lives in us (see Galatians 2:20). When we allow Christ to live in us and through us, then the being and doing of our liturgical spirituality meld into one. The self-emptying and Life-receiving of the paschal mystery truly are then a way of life, a spirituality that is the very core of who we are. As we embrace liturgical spirituality, our baptismal identity and commitment become more visible to others. We, then, are both a mirror of and witness to Christ's redeeming love. Liturgical spirituality is uncovered by our inherent goodness, by our love and care for others, and by the infectious joy that we exude.

Chapter 3: To Review and Reflect

Liturgical spirituality flows from and to the liturgy in such a way that liturgy informs our daily living.

- Holiness is a gift of living liturgical spirituality in that . . .
- The being of living liturgical spirituality is . . .
  The doing of liturgical spirituality is . . .
- Living from liturgical spirituality calls me to these ministries . . .

Liturgical spirituality is expressed in a daily, weekly, and yearly paschal mystery rhythm of celebration and living.

- My daily prayer looks like . . . I need to . . .
- I celebrate Sunday in these ways . . .
- I can become more aware of the seasons of the liturgical year if I were to . . .

From this chapter, I wish to remember . . .

4

DISCIPLESHIP EMBRACED

Prior to the mid-1960s and the Second Vatican Council, discipleship was hardly on the minds of the lay baptized. If they thought of it at all, it was in the context of the disciples mentioned in the New Testament. Vatican II radically changed that by reshaping the structure of ecclesial (Church) life. To be sure, the Council retained a hierarchical structure, but one based in the unity of the whole Church as the Body of Christ. Church is no longer a closed entity of those in authority and the rest of the people who have little to do with Church, except to fulfill sacramental and other obligations. Now the Church's fundamental issue is not turned in on itself (sanctification of the people and governance by the hierarchy), but is turned outward toward the whole world and the needs of people. The Church, at this time, is turned toward missionary activity by the activity of the Holy Spirit in each baptized member. The language of the Council was *apostolate*, a word obviously derived from *apostle*, referring to one sent as God's messenger to spread the Good News of salvation.

The popes since Vatican II have all used the term *evangelization*. The term comes from the Greek word for *Gospel*; we are used to calling the four Gospel writers "evangelists." In 2013, Pope Francis issued the apostolic exhortation *Evangelii gaudium* (*The Joy of the Gospel*), which addresses three groups: believers, those who are lukewarm about their faith, and nonbelievers (see no. 11; see also no. 15). In the exhortation, he calls for a new evangelization; he is calling for a new energy and enthusiasm about spreading the Gospel. Pope Francis was summoning everyone to a new way of living. He is not calling us to be preachers; he is calling us to live the Gospel in such a way that others are taken in by the goodness of our lives. The most profound preaching—evangelizing—is Gospel living. It is living a liturgical spirituality in such a way that others see Jesus' saving mission unfolding in the self-emptying and Life-receiving rhythm of the paschal mystery. To be a disciple is, first and foremost, to live a liturgical spirituality.

The starting point for the new evangelization is to take seriously our baptismal commitment to be a disciple. A disciple is a learner, and Jesus Christ is the One from whom we learn. Jesus Christ must become the very center of our lives. He must be our inspiration, stimulus, and encouragement in all we are and do. To be a disciple of the risen Christ means that we learn our way of life from his way of life. Unfortunately, the sad and misguided belief that religious education concludes with the celebration of the sacrament of confirmation still circulates in far too many communities. Not one sacrament, especially confirmation, should be seen as the "ticket out of" or completion of our religious formation. No, there is always a need for ongoing formation, not just in doctrine but in new ways of living and witnessing to our faith. We are dealing with mystery, so we can never understand everything; there can never be a time when we cease to be learners, cease to be disciples.

Discipleship is exercised first simply in daily Christian living, as the new evangelization stresses. It is not an "add on" to our daily life, but an expression of who we are as members of the Body of Christ. We learn from prayer and liturgy; we learn from observing the many good ways people live; we learn by mirroring in our lives the self-giving love that totally characterized Jesus' life. To be a disciple is to live the paschal mystery, to live a liturgical spirituality. Disciples so conform their lives to Christ that his way of living—self-giving for the sake of others—is our way of living. His dying and rising is our dying and rising. To say it another way: To be a disciple is to embrace, live, and mirror a liturgical spirituality that is a way of living patterned after Jesus' dying and rising.

We are both apostles (having been sent) and disciples (having been called to learn). The two go hand in hand. Our learning is so that we can be sent by the risen Christ—by the Church—to others. We sometimes forget that we human beings are social beings who exist in any number of communities: family, work, social clubs, Church, and so on. It is to all these communities that we witness our baptismal commitment to live as Jesus lived. We witness simply by being who we are, most particularly when we are faithful to Jesus' way of living. To witness to the Presence of Christ and the life to which he calls us demands our ongoing conversion. We constantly strive to learn more so that we can live more deeply goodness, mercy, forgiveness, compassion, and love. Since Gospel living is grounded in the mystery that Jesus' saving ministry is, we can never say our learning is complete. We can never say our growing is complete. We can never say that we have grasped the mystery and that conversion is complete. No, never!

Sometimes a commitment to the new evangelization can be exhausting; sometimes we best evangelize when we are not even aware of how our life and actions are affecting others in good ways. In order to meet the demands of Gospel living, we must be aware of the needs and signs of the times, become more cognizant of the Holy Spirit's Presence guiding us, and be gentle with ourselves when it seems like we are not growing in our Christian living. The demands of Gospel living are many, but not so overwhelming that each of us cannot make a difference in our Church, society, and world. Embracing discipleship is a matter of surrendering ourselves to be the risen Christ for others.

The Demands of Living the Gospel

The paschal mystery, liturgy, liturgical spirituality, and Gospel living fundamentally have the same demands and challenges. While there may be specific nuances of each of these realities, they all share our baptismal call to conform ourselves to Christ, upon whom we are grafted. We do not embrace our discipleship in name or words alone; true discipleship is a lived reality. We "preach" the Gospel by living the Gospel. We "preach" the Gospel through embracing liturgical spirituality, making liturgy the center of our lives.

> We "preach" the Gospel by living the Gospel. We "preach" the Gospel through embracing liturgical spirituality, making liturgy the center of our lives.

The basic demand of living the Gospel is to love one another as Jesus has loved us (see John 13:34). The key word here is *as*. Jesus is the prototype for our love. His loving is new; it is a divine love. His commandment to love is new because it is grounded in the life of the divine-human Son of God. This new commandment Jesus gives us is even more than the love that the Old Testament records for us.

THE NEW COMMANDMENT OF LOVE

Sometimes we hear that the God of the Old Testament is a vengeful God. Yes, much of that Scripture addresses sin and punishment; Israel found fidelity to God's commandments a difficult challenge, and often did not live up to the challenge. What we do not hear about often enough is the genuine, tender, faithful love that God showered upon the beloved People, even when they strayed from their covenantal fidelity. The prophet Hosea, for example, points to Israel's infidelity when God asks Hosea to marry Gomer, an unfaithful wife (see Hosea 1:2–3). Marriage to Hosea did not change Gomer's ways—she continued in her adulterous ways. She became the symbol for Israel, the unfaithful People beloved by God. God is the jealous Lover who cannot give up on Israel. Chapter 11 is a beautiful testimony to the tender and deep love that God bestows on Israel. The Song of Songs is an extended love poem depicting how God relentlessly pursues God's beloved Israel. Many other passages in the Old Testament teach us the same lesson: God loves us!

But Jesus' new commandment goes beyond even this demonstration of God's deep and abiding love. Jesus' command is to love as he loves. How did Jesus love? Unconditionally. Jesus loved with total self-giving, self-emptying, and self-surrender; he loved by looking beyond face value and seeing the goodness in everyone whom he encountered; he loved by responding to anyone in need without judgment. This kind of generous love is unprecedented. Jesus excludes no one, is recoiled by no one, is afraid of no one. His love challenges us to expand our community relations beyond what is known and familiar and creatively grasp every opportunity to encounter another by being his risen Presence.

Jesus' love is not a naive love. It makes demands on us as it did on him. Like him, we will be misunderstood, tested, made to suffer. Like him, we need to die to ourselves in order to be free to reach out to all those whose paths cross ours. But also like him, we share in risen Life. Like him, we will pass over from death to risen Life. But Jesus' time and culture were very different from ours. To be his faithful disciples today, we must be able to read the needs and signs of the times.

NEEDS AND SIGNS OF THE TIMES

Pete Seeger recorded "Turn, Turn, Turn" in 1959, and since then several artists have also recorded it. The lyrics are a take on the Old Testament Book of Ecclesiastes (3:1–8) that addresses the vagaries and contrasts in human life, insisting that there is a time and season for everything. Sorting out values in human life and judgment in face of them takes ongoing discernment. Each era has its own challenges. In order to embrace fruitful discipleship, we must be attuned to the needs and signs of the times. Jesus himself showed us the way; he was so very tuned into the people and needs around him. He reminded his hearers that they could predict rain coming when observing clouds forming or that it will be warm when the wind blows from the south. He admonishes them: If they can read these weather signs, why cannot they see what is happening in their own time and context (see Luke 12:54–56)? This being attuned enabled him to meet people where they were and to minister to them in their concrete need.

The last document approved by Vatican II was a pastoral constitution addressing the needs and signs of the time. While the document points to many ills in society, its title *Gaudium et spes*, "joy and hope," offers us encouragement while at the same time the constitution challenges us. Discipleship must be real; it must meet people where they are with their needs and concerns, their hopes and aspirations, their anguish and sorrows. Living the Gospel means we open our eyes to the real situation in which we find ourselves—not only in our own neighborhoods and towns, but in the whole world. Just think of all that has happened in our world since December 1965! But first let us reflect on the half-century-ago context of this important document.

Gaudium et spes is not shy about pointing to the needs of its time. The constitution mentions a deep "spiritual uneasiness" (no. 5) that has crept in, not a small part of which is the result of advances in science and a scientific mentality. It mentions the effects on society with the breakdown of traditional structures such as family units (no. 6). It mentions changes in attitudes and morals (no. 7) and imbalances and tensions arising from socio-economic structures, racism, cultural conflicts, and nationalism (no. 8). At the same time it upholds our dignity as those created in the image of God (nos. 12, 15–17); it speaks of the common good (nos. 25–26), respect (nos. 27–28), and equality (no. 29). And so much more. In short, *Gaudium et spes* challenges us to discern the needs of our time and respond with joy and hope, helping our world reflect the Presence of God's reign.

In the mid-1960s, the Second Vatican Council could hardly have imagined the world we live in and are making as we journey through the twenty-first century. Neil Armstrong had yet to take that first step on the moon (July 1969). Personal computers, smart phones, and so much technology were the things of science fiction. The internet did not exist. Face-to-face, in-the-moment conversations with people all around the world could not have been imagined. The world had not shrunk to the point where all of us are neighbors. Our world society today calls for creative and new responses for those who wish to be disciples following Jesus' very concrete responses to his society.

Just about every advancement today has both pluses and minuses. Our challenge as disciples is to bring Gospel values into our choices around using the technology and science and information that is available to us. Different people have different needs; our challenge is to separate needs from wants, to be aware that when we have too much someone else may be deprived, to use what we have for the good of others, to strive for moral truth in all we do. Gospel living demands that we always place ourselves and our preferences within the context of the community of persons with whom we daily interact. We do not exist in isolation, but in relation to others. Jesus told his disciples that he did not come to relate to them as slaves, but as friends (see John 15:15). As his disciples, we are friends to others when we give ourselves over to them for their good as Jesus did for those in his time.

The demands of living the Gospel for us are no less than those on Jesus. He showed us the way to be aware of others' needs, of others' anguish, of others' seeming inadequacies. He did so by meeting others where they were, by not judging them but by listening and responding and loving. Each encounter with each individual demands a different Gospel response. There is no simple blueprint for responding to others in loving service. But Jesus knew the cost of the demands and made sure we would not be alone in our struggle to be faithful. He promised the Holy Spirit to teach us all we need (see John 14:26) to be disciple-witnesses to the risen Christ. With the Holy Spirit guiding us, the demands of living the Gospel become our joy and hope.

> The demands of living the Gospel for us are no less than those on Jesus.

THE HOLY SPIRIT'S PRESENCE GUIDING US

How comforting to know that we are not on our own in accepting and living our discipleship. The gift of the Holy Spirit, first received at baptism, is no small gift, indeed. In both the Apostles' and Nicene Creeds we profess that we believe in the Holy Spirit. It is only by the Spirit's indwelling that we can bear fruit in our discipleship (see CCC, 736). Through the Spirit we are able to continue Jesus' saving mission. How so? Openness to the Spirit's promptings guides us through our decision-making, helps us make right judgments, and leads us truly along our journey of life in Christ. The challenge is to look for and recognize the Spirit's promptings in our daily lives.

Since the Sacred Scriptures are the inspired Word of God, one way to open ourselves to the Spirit's guidance is to take sufficient time to read and pray with the Sacred Scriptures. A traditional spiritual practice that has gained much acceptance and practice lately is *lectio divina* (divine reading). The point of *lectio* is not to get through as many verses or chapters of Scripture as we can at a time. The point is to read Scripture and then, when some word or phrase pops out, to stop, reflect, and pray with those words. It helps to read Scripture aloud to ourselves so we can, so to speak, "hear" the voice of the Holy Spirit. It demands self-discipline to make *lectio divina* a daily spiritual exercise. We need to slow down our sacred reading so that we can truly listen to the voice of the Spirit. We need to allow our hearts to spill over into prayer for help, for guidance, and for inspiration.

Another way to become aware of the Holy Spirit guiding us is to pay attention to what happens to us during the day. The age-old spiritual practice of making an examination of conscience at the end of our day is a helpful tool. This focused prayer helps us become aware of our faults and failings during the past day so that we can do better the next day.

Greater openness to the Holy Spirit's guidance can be realized by adding another practice to our daily examination of conscience: recalling all the blessings we have received during the day. Blessings come from God; becoming aware of them is a gift of the Holy Spirit. The Holy Spirit fills the whole world (see CCC, 11), leads us to goodness, and orients us toward to fullness of Life that the risen Christ promises.

Many people earnest about growing in their spiritual life seek spiritual direction. This, too, is an age-old practice. A spiritual mentor (the advisor or director) listens to the one desiring to learn more about the Holy Spirit's Presence and guidance in life; the mentor helps the individual recognize the Spirit's activity and encourages the individual in spiritual growth. As the sharing unfolds, the fruits of one's discipleship become very evident. New directions are often discovered. New possibilities are encouraged. New prayer methods are tried. Opening oneself up to another is not always easy; it demands trust, inner security, honesty, integrity, and a willingness to be vulnerable. The consolation during the hard work of spiritual growth is the abiding Presence and guidance of the Holy Spirit.

Be Gentle with Ourselves

As our desire to be faithful to the Gospel living required of discipleship grows, it is easy to become discouraged, especially when we don't feel the Spirit's Presence and guidance, when we can't see growth in the Gospel quality of our daily living, and when we aren't able to recognize the fruits of our discipleship. Some of the great mystics in our Church's history wrote about a "dark night of the soul." Spiritual growth is not usually a simple, steady movement forward. Often, we can feel empty, our prayer doesn't seem to satisfy or give joy, or we can even feel abandoned by God. These feelings might last a few days, months, or even years. We must be gentle with ourselves. We must humbly admit that, just as Jesus faced suffering, so will we as we embrace his way of living. Jesus wrestled with the temptations in the desert before he embarked on his public ministry (see Matthew 4:11). Jesus anguished in the Garden the night before he was betrayed, begging his Father to take the impending cup of suffering and death away from him (see Luke 22:41–42). But note that the context of this suffering was prayer. This is a good lesson. When we forget to be gentle with ourselves, when we grow impatient with our seeming lack of spiritual growth, when we are tempted to give up, we need to join with Jesus in his prayer, confident that his Spirit will refresh us and carry us forward to the fruits of faithful Gospel living.

The Fruits of Living the Gospel

We can do nothing without God's help. In particular, the Holy Spirit is given to us at baptism to guide us, to help us come closer to the risen Christ so we can live his life and continue his ministry; the Spirit inspires us to live the Gospel. Living a Spirit-Life fills us with the very Presence of God. No matter what turmoil life might throw our way, when we are open to this divine Presence, virtue and tranquility abound.

The Letter to the Galatians names specific fruits of the Holy Spirit given as we surrender ourselves to God's way of living: love, joy, peace, patience, kindness, generosity, faithfulness, gentleness, self-control (see Galatians 5:22–23). To these nine fruits of the Holy Spirit are added three more in the tradition of the Church: goodness, modesty, and chastity (see CCC, 1832; the fruits given in Galatians 5:22–23 are those listed in CCC no. 736). These fruits are gifts that are bestowed as we continually grow in grafting ourselves onto Christ. They contrast with self-indulgent living that leads to sinfulness—a weakening of or destroying our relationship to God.

The fruits of the Holy Spirit are gifts given us so that we can see beyond any difficulty, challenge, or suffering that come our way as we choose to do God's will in our daily living. They do not do away with events and people that are problematic for us. They do not take away pain or suffering. But, as with the paschal mystery, we know that the dying always includes rising. We know that self-emptying always includes Life-receiving. Living the Gospel is essentially living liturgical spirituality. And liturgical spirituality carries us through death to new Life, through hardship to the fruits of the Holy Spirit that are indications of our conformity to Christ.

All these fruits, one way or another, point to fulfilling relationships with God, others, and self. Gospel living—surrendering ourselves to the way Jesus lived—deepens these fruits, and in turn enables us to ever more faithful Gospel living. As we grow, we deepen the quality of our relationships in the Body of Christ. These fruits are the confirmation of the good choices we make every day to follow in the footsteps of Jesus. These fruits of the Holy Spirit are the gift of faithful discipleship, of which Jesus' Mother Mary is the first and most ardent disciple of her divine Son.

Mary as a Model of Discipleship

Mary, the Mother of God and the Mother of the Church, is a perfect daughter of God to whom we might look for guidance in our discipleship living. Mary is the first disciple, even before Jesus' birth. She unreservedly said yes to God's invitation to be the mother of the divine Son (see Luke 1:38). She could not possibly have known what this yes would entail. Yet she surrendered. She gave the first (wordless) testimony of the Presence of the Savior at her encounter with Elizabeth, who, recognizing that Mary was carrying Jesus in her womb, was filled with the Holy Spirit (see Luke 1:42). Even John the Baptist in Elizabeth's womb leaped at this divine-human encounter (see Luke 1:41).

During Jesus' "hidden life," Mary would have been both teacher (apostle) and learner (disciple). She taught Jesus by her own exemplary life of virtue and fidelity—no doubt fed by her relationship to her God. At the wedding feast at Cana, she exhibited compassion, command, and confidence that her divine Son would do as she wished (see John 2:11); she learned of his generous power used to ease others' lives. Throughout what we know of her life, Mary relates to more people than only her divine Son. At Jesus' birth, she receives the shepherds and Magi (see Luke 2:16 and Matthew 2:11). Upon leaving the wedding at Cana, she is in the midst of disciples and travels with them (see John 2:12). She is present at the crucifixion, when as one of the last acts of her divine Son, she was given the beloved disciple John as her son and to John as his mother (see John 19:26–27). We do not know whether Jesus appeared to Mary after the resurrection; however, it seems inconceivable that he would not make his risen Presence known to his mother. What a reunion that must have been! Mary stayed close to the disciples and was

> Without understanding God's ways fully, Mary surrendered herself and remained faithful. She trusted in God. A disciple trusts the One from whom we learn.

present in the Upper Room awaiting Pentecost (see Acts 1:14 and 2:1–4). Mary can never be separated from the Church, the Body of Christ; she is our mother, and we can learn much from her.

Mary's virtues teach us the characteristics of being a faithful disciple of her divine Son. She was full of grace (see Luke 1:28) and remained close to Jesus, not being shielded from the bitter pains of rejection, misjudgment, and condemnation that he would accept. She was called by God to cooperate in the divine mission of salvation and remained open to God's will for her. Her life focused on her divine Son; while there are few Scripture passages that speak of Mary, all of them are in relation to her Son and his saving mission. Mary had a contemplative spirit, indicated by her pondering things in her heart (see Luke 1:29 and 2:19), and prayer was easily on her lips; when she visited her cousin Elizabeth, who called her "blessed," Mary spoke words of praise to God, words that are prayed every day throughout the world in the Evening Prayer of the Church (see the Magnificat, the Canticle of Mary, Luke 1:46–55). Mary was not afraid to ask questions and to seek clarification, as she did with Gabriel at the Annunciation (see Luke 1:34) and upon finding Jesus in the Temple (see Luke 2:48). Without understanding God's ways fully, Mary surrendered herself and remained faithful. She trusted in God. A disciple trusts the One from whom we learn.

Mary understood well the self-emptying demands of discipleship and the fruits that are the effect of being faithful. In a way, Mary's whole life was a liturgy: she participated fully and unconditionally in her divine Son's death and resurrection. She lived in constant divine Presence and encounter. She is the first disciple, and the first to model liturgical spirituality. From the very beginning of her life, she was in communion with her Beloved. She lived her life faithfully by learning his ways. She surrendered herself to him. She lived through her sorrows to the glory promised and in which she now shares for eternity. This is the way of a disciple.

The Holy Spirit and Gifts We Have Received

Mary is a very exalted model of discipleship and liturgical spirituality. After all, she was highly favored by God (see Luke 1:28). She bore the divine Son. She had a most intimate, mother's relationship with him. How can we possibly step up to this model? On our own, we cannot. But the risen Christ, in his infinite divine wisdom, did not leave us without an Advocate. He sends the Holy Spirit to dwell within and among us. At baptism each of us receives the Holy Spirit and the gifts that the Spirit bestows. It is these gifts that empower us to take from Mary the encouragement and discipline we need to be faithful to Gospel living. The Holy Spirit overshadows us as that same Spirit overshadowed Mary. We, too, bear the risen Christ within.

The Holy Spirit is the divine Person proceeding from the dynamic Love of the Father and Son. Love begets all. The Greek term *perichoresis* (to dance through) captures well the inner dynamism of the Holy Trinity. The love of the Three Persons is so vibrant that the Three are truly One. *Perichoresis* is a divine dance whereby the interpenetrating movements of the Persons of the Holy Trinity are joyfully Life-giving to each other; this divine Life that cannot be contained, is given to us. Grace is the indwelling Presence of Holy Spirit and a share in divine Life. Because of that Presence, we receive the gifts and fruits of the Holy Spirit. The Holy Spirit makes us holy, of God; as grace deepens, so do the fruits and gifts showered upon us. There are traditionally seven gifts of the Holy Spirit: wisdom, understanding, counsel, fortitude, knowledge, piety, and fear (awe) of the Lord (see CCC, 1831; also 1845).

The first five gifts on the list are clearly directed to giving us the tools to be disciples continuing Jesus' work of salvation. Briefly, wisdom helps us glean the deeper meaning, hidden treasures, and sublime harmonies of the truths of our faith. Understanding assists us in grasping the truth of our belief, commitment, and orientation to God. Counsel prompts us to seek others' help and make proper judgments about what is right for us, sometimes quickly in difficult and demanding situations. Fortitude shores up our courage to resist temptation and shoulder the difficult tasks that confront us. Knowledge aids us in grasping divine truths even though they remain mysteries. These gifts fortify our liturgical spirituality because they draw us to the depths of the mystery we celebrate at liturgy.

The last two gifts of the Holy Spirit are clearly directed to our relationship with God. Piety prompts us to be devoted to God and God's ways. It is a habit of the soul that is observable in the glory of holiness, the deep communion we have with God and all others; it aids us in turning to God in all things. Piety is a gift that helps us connect the ritual of liturgy to the daily living of liturgy; in other words, piety helps us comprehend how liturgical spirituality unfolds in our daily journey with Christ. The fear of the Lord does not mean being terrified of God so that we make choices out of the fright of being punished. Rather, this gift is a help in understanding that we fear God out of love rather than loving God out of fear. Fear of the Lord is born out of a deep humility that arises from shear awe of God's greatness, and the unbelievable gift of God that is a share in divine Life. Fear of God awakens in us a deep awe of God's nearness, God's blessings, and God's love.

Discipleship is not daunting when we consider how God equips us to continue the divine Son's saving mission. Will hardships occur? Absolutely. Will we be discouraged at times? Absolutely. Will the journey of discipleship sometimes seem beyond us? Absolutely. When these times happen, we need to gently bring ourselves back to the rhythm of liturgical spirituality. We are never left to die as if that is all there is. Jesus has overcome death (see 2 Timothy 1:10). By dying to self, we conform ourselves more perfectly to the risen Christ and, in this grafting of ourselves onto him, we live. Death did not conquer Jesus; he rose. Neither will death conquer us; we will also rise to the fullness of Life. Our own dying to self as we continue Jesus' saving mission is a pledge of the risen Life that Jesus already shares with us. The Holy Spirit ensures that we have all we need to come to full stature in Christ as his Body here and now. The gifts of the Holy Spirit ensure that we are equipped to face any challenge or demand that we disciples might encounter. Embracing discipleship means that we surrender ourselves to the Holy Spirit and allow those gifts work through us. We are not disciples alone; the Holy Spirit is within and among us.

In the introduction, the question we posed to be addressed in this final chapter was, Why is liturgical spirituality demanding, but at the same time encouraging, in that we are not alone in this way of living? Liturgical spirituality is demanding because it entails giving ourselves over as Jesus did and as Mary did. The demand is to surrender ourselves to something larger than ourselves, to something we do not fully understand because it is mystery, to Someone who sometimes seems far away. But in this never-ending challenge, there is faith, hope, and love. We are never alone; the Spirit dwells within us to guide and strengthen us.

Discipleship is to learn from a master; disciples of Jesus are to learn from the Master, the divine Son who came to reveal his Father (see Matthew 11:27). Jesus promised that he will walk in tandem with us, our yoke is his yoke (see Matthew 11:29). In him we rest. In him our discipleship will come to fruition. In him we have Life eternal.

Chapter 4: to Review and Reflect

To be a disciple is to be a learner.

- I learn best from the risen Christ when . . .
- The relationship between being a disciple and meeting the demands of Gospel living is . . .
- I am most often encouraged in my faithful discipleship when . . .

The new commandment Jesus revealed is that we should love as he loves us.

- The Holy Spirit's gifts and fruits help me fulfill the new commandment of love in that . . .
- Mary is a model of the new commandment in love and inspires me to . . .
- The gifts I have received from the Holy Spirit to build up the Body of Christ are . . .

From this chapter, I wish to remember . . .

Concluding Remarks

Liturgical spirituality is a matter of journeying daily with Christ in his saving mystery, and this is sometimes easy and sometimes challenging. It is easy when we remember that liturgy is our anchor. No matter what our frame of mind when we come to liturgy, the ritual will carry us. When we assemble and surrender ourselves as individuals to being the whole Body of Christ, the Church made visible, we are together with others in community. They carry us and we carry them. The fruits of liturgy are not dependent upon our readiness, but only on our surrender to letting God work in and through us. In daily living, after we are dismissed from liturgy to live what we have celebrated, we hopefully often have good days of living liturgical spirituality. On the other hand, journeying daily with Christ can be challenging when choices with which we are faced are contrary to Gospel values. It can be challenging when some days we just do not take the time to be attentive to God in prayer to learn the divine will for us. It can be challenging when we lose sight of Christ at the center of our lives, of the Holy Spirit's guidance and strength, of God's compassion and forgiveness.

We have reflected on the paschal mystery as a rhythm of self-emptying and Life-receiving that is enacted in liturgy and played out in our daily journey with Christ as liturgical spirituality. We experience this rhythm in the daily, weekly, and yearly unfolding of rites and year. As we grow in liturgical spirituality—a way of living flowing from and to the paschal rhythm of liturgy—this rhythm more and more begins to become the good habit of centering everything on Christ and his saving mystery that determines how we approach each day. As we frame our days, weeks, and years by the paschal mystery, we more and more take on as our spirituality the reality of our immersion at baptism into the saving ministry of Jesus.

Liturgy is the fount from which this rhythm flows and deepens; it is the summit to which we return so we do not forget who and Whose we are. When we make liturgy the fount and summit of our Gospel living,

> The fruits of liturgy are not dependent upon our readiness, but only on our surrender to letting God work in and through us.

we have opened ourselves to lives defined by a liturgical way of living; that is, we have established liturgical spirituality as our way of living. This liturgical spirituality, in turn, shapes our discipleship. Our Gospel living looks and becomes more and more the way Jesus himself lived. Liturgical spirituality as a way of living is the root of all our relationships, the determiner of all our choices, and the anchor on which we rely when life becomes confusing or stressful or seemingly unbearable.

As we grow in paschal mystery living, in deepening the joy of liturgical celebrations, in more confidence in our discipleship, we know we have accepted and nurtured our liturgical spirituality. Practice in celebrating liturgy and living daily the rhythm of the paschal mystery helps form a good habit of embracing discipleship as expressing nothing less than liturgical spirituality. We grasp the beauty and richness of the reality of the risen Christ's abiding Presence within and among us. And oh what joy we have when we can say, as did St. Paul, I no longer live but Christ lives in me (see Galatians 2:20)!

APPENDIX:
Spirituality of Liturgical Ministers

In the four chapters of our reflection on liturgical spirituality, we have focused on a spirituality that is for everyone who is baptized. It is a way of living that flows from our baptismal commitment to be disciples of the risen Christ. It is a way of living that makes the celebration of liturgy the center of our lives. Liturgical spirituality is a way of life for all the baptized who are eager to grow in their relationship to the risen Christ and continue his saving ministry.

Some people volunteer to take on the responsibilities of the various ministries needed for liturgy to unfold in a beautiful and timely manner. These special liturgical ministries are not jobs that are simply performed or done but are special ministries specific to a particular liturgy (for example, Sunday Mass, baptism, and Liturgy of the Hours). To fulfil a ministry that truly serves the assembled community, these special liturgical ministers also have an underlying spirituality, which they must nurture. For them—as well as all of us—living a liturgical spirituality, the doing, must flow from their being. It is not in addition to the liturgical spirituality distinguishing those baptized into Christ but it specifies more directly how these ministers live their liturgical spirituality in order that they might minister more effectively during liturgy.

This appendix offers some thoughts on the spirituality appropriate for nine particular liturgical ministries. The last three ministries (music ministry, hospitality ministry, and service ministry) include several different kinds of ministries having a common theme. Most parishes would have all these liturgical ministries, some more formal and visible than others. While parishes regularly tend to liturgical ministry formation, this learning tends to focus on the "nuts and bolts," on the various tasks of each ministry. It is good to add a spiritual dimension, the being, to liturgical ministry formation. It is in this spirit that these further reflections are offered. To keep these considerations more focused, we concentrate on how these liturgical ministries occur during Mass. In many cases, what is said here would apply to other liturgical celebrations and also to communal devotional prayer.

Spirituality of the Ministry of the Assembly

The Being and Doing of the Ministry of the Assembly

We do far more when we come together for liturgy than simply get together for a common action. The *being* of the liturgical assembly is to be Church made visible. The ordained priest is in our midst as the Head of the Body, the visible Presence of Christ. When we gather as one, Head and Body, we are Church. The *doing* of the assembly is to surrender ourselves as individual members of the Body of Christ to being the one Body of Christ that is larger than ourselves as individuals. All our full, conscious, active participation in liturgy is directed to becoming more perfectly the Body of Christ.

The Role of the Assembly

The liturgical assembly manifests the Church, the Body of Christ, in its fullness. Every person who gathers for liturgy is a minister to self and others. As liturgical assembly, the gathered people—ordained priest and people, Head and Body—enact the paschal mystery and continue Christ's ongoing work of salvation. When we gather as liturgical assembly, we call to mind and live out our identity and mission. We renew our baptismal commitment to being disciples of the risen Christ, connect with liturgical spirituality in the very shape of the liturgy, and are sent forth to be the Presence of Christ to all those we meet.

Characteristics of the Spirituality of the Ministry of the Assembly

- *Communal.* Communion with other members of the Body of Christ reveals the many gifts given to the community to continue Jesus' saving ministry. No one of us has all the necessary qualities and talents to continue Jesus' saving mission. Together, we have all we need when we surrender ourselves to continue Jesus' mission. The spirituality of the ministry of the assembly calls us in our daily living to overcome divisions and promote unity.

- *Universal.* One of the four marks of the Church is that it is *catholic*, that is, universal. The liturgical assembly is not just a collection of individuals gathered at a certain time and place. The liturgical assembly is far-reaching: It encompasses the whole Church, past, present, and future. It is the visible presence of the communion of saints offering God praise and thanks. As such, each member of the liturgical assembly is a model of welcome for anyone who comes and for anyone who is met in the daily circumstances of life.

- *Other-centered.* Selfishness has no place in members of the liturgical assembly. Like Christ our Head, the members of the assembly strive to be all things to all people. No one is excluded, everyone has the dignity of the children of God, others' needs are our own needs. The surrender proper to becoming a liturgical assembly mirrors the kind of surrender to the care of others that is part and parcel of our daily Christian living.

- *Open to surrendering.* Our natural tendency is to be concerned about ourselves. This is appropriate and necessary for us to have what we need to live a good life. We tend to keep what is ours. Contrary to this, the ministry of the assembly requires us to let go of ourselves—to surrender our thoughts and desires, preferences and habits, likes and dislikes to become more than we are as individuals. Without our being open to surrendering to the liturgical action, we block God's desire to transform us into more perfect images of the divine Presence.

- *All focus on common identity united under one Head.* Variety in our liturgical assembly is indicative of no one being excluded from God's Beloved People. What draws this variety into a seamless whole is a concerted focus on Christ, who is Head of the Body and who unites us as one. We assemble in response to Christ's call; it is Christ who is the reason for our being and doing, and the cause of our becoming a community united in one purpose.

- *Accepting of diversity.* A variety of gifts and people make up the liturgical assembly. To celebrate liturgy well we must recognize each one's place and role in the immense diversity that characterizes our liturgical assembly. Everyone has something to contribute, and the differences simply help us grasp the creativity of God in the variety of people gathered.

- *Real commitment to celebrating "good" liturgy.* It is very easy to get lost in our personal likes and dislikes about how liturgy ought to unfold. We must be willing to be formed in what good liturgy is and why the Church is so particular about how liturgy is celebrated. Liturgy is not our personal prayer, although there are times during liturgical rites that allow us personal prayer. Liturgy is a communal prayer of the whole Church and, as such, every liturgical assembly must be willing to know, understand, and be formed in the liturgy as it is most fruitfully celebrated.

- *Balances liturgical and devotional prayer.* Liturgical prayer cannot be the only prayer of the members of the assembly. If we never raise our minds and hearts to God during daily living, then nothing magic will happen at liturgy in encountering God. Our own daily, personal prayer is a kind of "practice" in opening ourselves to God's Presence, encountering God in divine goodness, and listening for the direction God wishes us to take in our daily living.

APPROPRIATING THIS SPIRITUALITY

- One concrete behavior I choose to do in my daily living to deepen the spirituality of this ministry for me is . . .

- One concrete action I choose to do to enhance the effectiveness of my ministry is . . .

Spirituality of the Ministry of the Presider

The Being and Doing of the Ministry of the Presider

We cannot have the Eucharistic celebration without an ordained priest. This, because the *being* of the ministry of the presider is to be the visible Presence of Christ, the Head of the Church. He usually is last in the entrance procession, and this is symbolic. When he reaches the presider's chair, the assembly is complete—that is, the Church is complete: Head united with the Body of Christ. The *doing* of this ministry is to relate to the rest of the assembly as Christ; he is in the midst of the Church leading all of us to the banquet of word and sacrament.

The Role of the Presider

The presider is the one who leads the assembly in prayer. To this end, he pays special attention to the dynamic unfolding within the prayer, paces its flow, "reads" the assembly. By his prayerful leading he sets the tone for the whole celebration. If the prayer leader himself is truly praying, chances are that the assembly will more easily be drawn into the liturgy as prayer. Everything about the presider's persona is to speak to the assembly about the solemnity of what we do together. There is no greater privilege for the baptized than to be in the Presence of God and together enacting the paschal mystery. The presider must take care in all he does, and do everything with grace and beauty, purpose and reverence, fidelity, and joy.

Characteristics of the Spirituality of the Ministry of the Presider

The presider is one who respects the prayer of the whole assembly while he leads the prayer. It is never appropriate for the presider to impose his personal piety on an assembly. The celebration style needs to be common to all. Some special characteristics:

- *Be himself.* No two priests are alike, so it is natural to expect some personality differences in the way each priest presides. However, personalities ought not to get in the way of doing as the Church wishes. Idiosyncratic use of voice, gestures, dress, movement, eye contact and so forth are generally distractive and take the focus of the participants away from the liturgical action. But certainly, priests are expected to be themselves and be comfortable in a celebration style that is somewhat unique to them. While being himself, he never draws attention to self.

- *Faith filled and committed.* The priest's love of the Church, of ministering to the people, of leading them in this most sacred act can be shown in many ways. He is to be reverent, gentle, charitable, prayerful, and convey a sense of the mystery he is celebrating. It is a challenge for priests who preside at multiple liturgies on a given day to stay fresh and prayerful. It helps to remember that for the people assembled, this is most likely their one liturgy of the day.

- *Sense of being a member of assembly.* The priest leads the assembly, but he is not apart from the assembly. This precludes any sense of being better than other assembly members, being served rather than serving, being comfortable with how to lead but not distancing himself from the others present. This is not an issue of spatial distancing (it is appropriate that the presider's chair be apart from the assembly seating), but of spiritual inclusion in the one assembly.

- *Attentive to both local and universal Church.* Liturgy is always the liturgy of the whole Church, but there are marked differences among different local communities and even among different celebrations of a single parish. While, for example, the *General Instruction of the Roman Missal* (see no. 70) gives four categories for the intentions of the Universal Prayer (Prayer of the Faithful), it would be remiss for a presider to ignore something that is happening locally that the assembly ought to remember in their prayer; it is appropriate, then, to include an additional intention.

- *Openness to others.* The presider's ministry is a "service" of leadership. He is there for others. Consequently, he must have respect for the charisms of others, especially of other liturgical ministers. He must recognize the many different people who come together at any given celebration; indeed, inculturation is one of the biggest challenges facing those who prepare and minister at liturgy. He must be patient with the babies who are crying, with the disabled who may have extra needs, with the minister who forgets something. Sometimes something as simple as good eye contact can put others at ease.

- *Minister of the Church.* The presider has a huge responsibility in his being a minister of the whole Church. If he knows his own human limitations, he can more easily surrender himself to the sacred ministry he undertakes. He must be "at home" with what he is doing, must practice hospitality of self as well as with others. But his hospitality is not a matter of being "homey," but of welcoming and putting others at ease. He must practice "custody of the tongue," meaning that his own comments are made where permitted and appropriate, and he refrains from comments that are too lengthy or made too often, which would detract from the sacredness of the words of the celebration.

Appropriating This Spirituality

- ◇ One concrete behavior I choose to do in my daily living to deepen the spirituality of this ministry for me is . . .
- ◇ One concrete action I choose to do to enhance the effectiveness of my ministry is . . .

Spirituality of the Ministry of the Deacon

The Being and Doing of the Ministry of the Deacon

There is not always a deacon present at a Eucharistic celebration, but this does not mean the deacon does not have an important place at Mass. The *being* of the deacon is to be an icon of service; he is to make visible the kind of caring service to others that we all share as members of the Body of Christ. The *doing* of the deacon is to proclaim the Gospel, announce the intentions of the Universal Prayer (Prayer of the Faithful), and receive the assembly's gifts for the poor. All these actions point to his service role and his knowledge of the needs of the community.

The Role of the Deacon

The deacon is a servant of the community. He is a living reminder of our baptismal call to care for other members of the Body of Christ, especially those in most need. His three primary liturgical roles each point to his being a servant-minister. As the one who proclaims the Gospel, he is in a position to remind the people of what Gospel living looks like: caring for each other. As the one who announces the intentions at the Universal Prayer (Prayer of the Faithful), his service to the members of the community puts him in a position to know best what needs should be presented in prayer. By receiving the assembly's gifts for the poor, he is announcing to them, in his very person, his concern for those in need and reminds the assembly of their responsibility toward the less fortunate and anyone in need of assistance.

THE CHARACTERISTICS OF THE SPIRITUALITY OF THE MINISTRY OF THE DEACON

- *Genuine concern and care for others.* What the deacon does for others is not simply a job, but a ministry that arises from his being ordained to serve others in the community. While certain kinds of serving take skills, the most important kind of serving comes from a heart that is steeped in compassion, love, and caring.

- *Comfortable with loving others.* When we hear the word *love* we all too often conjure up a very limited expression of it as unadulterated emotion. The deacon's love is much more like Jesus' love: self-giving for the sake of others. The deacon's love excludes no one. It draws the community together in a bond of charity.

- *Observant of people.* The deacon cannot know the needs of others unless his eyes are open to them, observant of their condition in life. This means that the deacon must circulate within the community if he is to know its needs.

- *Generosity.* Basic to any fruitful service is the virtue of generosity. Kindness and compassion must become a habit so actions flowing from them become natural. Self-giving is a way of life for the deacon.

- *Good listener.* Sometimes the most important care someone needs is simply a listening ear. Listening is how a deacon becomes aware of the community's needs, discerns what an appropriate response is, and determines who might help in his service ministry.

- *Comfortable with different people and different tasks.* The deacon's service ministry can take on many forms, and often when he meets another who expresses a need, he might be surprised about what is asked of him. The deacon needs to be creative in his response to people, comfortable stretching himself beyond what he thinks his talents are, and not be afraid to take risks.

Appropriating This Spirituality

- One concrete behavior I choose to do in my daily living to deepen the spirituality of this ministry for me is . . .

- One concrete action I choose to do to enhance the effectiveness of my ministry is . . .

Spirituality of the Ministry of Acolyte and Altar Server

The Being and Doing of the Ministry of Acolyte and Altar Server

These ministers are called "acolytes" in some communities, and "altar servers" in others. In most dioceses they can be either boys or girls, men or women. All are called to live the spirituality of this ministry, although adults will no doubt have a more mature approach. The *being* of this ministry is to be a footprint of readiness and attentiveness. The *doing* of this ministry is to attend to any need the presider might have to fulfill his proper role of leading the community in liturgical prayer.

The Role of Acolyte and Altar Server

The acolyte or altar server is one who serves the presider and/or deacon; in this, ultimately, she or he serves the whole community. By ensuring that the liturgy unfolds with grace and facility, the acolyte promotes the dynamic of the rite. The acolyte is unobtrusive in ministry, in order that there be no diversion from the central action.

Characteristics of the Spirituality of the Ministry of Acolyte and Altar Server

- *Observant and aware.* Most of what is expected of the acolyte or altar server is the same for every Eucharistic celebration. But the acolyte must be aware of what is happening, observe when unexpected things happen, and be immediately ready to assist. If something else is happening at a particular celebration—for example, a baptism—she or he must be aware of what is expected.
- *Quiet, unobtrusive demeanor.* The acolyte does nothing to draw attention to himself or herself but is a kind of "hidden" minister.

The acolyte's gracious manner draws attention to the unfolding action and in a quiet and unobtrusive manner promotes a smooth movement of the ritual action from its beginning to its conclusion.

- *Other-centered.* The acolyte must be other-centered, focused on the presider's and others' needs. Other-centeredness draws the acolyte out of himself or herself so that he or she can anticipate when something else is needed or if something is missing that is necessary for the rite.

- *Ceremony with grace and ease.* Although the acolyte does this ministry unobtrusively, at the same time all the acolyte's actions need to be carried out deliberately, with grace and ease. The acolyte contributes to the unfolding beauty of the ritual action.

- *Knowledgeable about each ritual and its demands.* Eagerness to know and understand the details of various rites (especially those only occasionally celebrated such as the extra elements of weddings, funerals, and annual liturgies like Palm Sunday and the Easter Vigil) is essential if the acolyte is to fulfill this ministry well.

- *Purposeful.* Daydreaming is the bane of acolytes! They must be focused and purposeful, aware of each step of the rite and what comes next.

Appropriating This Spirituality

- One concrete behavior I choose to do in my daily living to deepen the spirituality of this ministry for me is . . .

- One concrete action I choose to do to enhance the effectiveness of my ministry is . . .

Spirituality of the Ministry of Lector

The Being and Doing of the Ministry of Lector

The lector does more than merely read words; the lector speaks God's Word in such a way that it is a living Word. The *being* of the lector is to be a visible word of God's will and purpose. The *doing* of the lector is to proclaim the Scriptures in such a way that it touches the hearts of those listening.

The Role of Lector

The lector is one who proclaims (not "reads") God's Word to the assembly. To this end, she or he must be a living word herself or himself; one cannot proclaim what one does not live. The Word burns within the heart of the lector so that, like the prophet Jeremiah (see Jeremiah 20:9), the lector is eager to proclaim the living Word of God. The lector approaches the ambo with respect and dignity and handles the lectionary with due honor.

Characteristics of the Spirituality of the Ministry of Lector

- *Regularly and often ponders God's Word.* It is not enough to prepare to proclaim only by looking at the readings to review or practice pronunciation. The lector must read and pray God's Word in such a way that the Word comes alive in the lector's heart and is lived in whatever daily tasks the lector assumes. Preparing to lector begins well before the liturgy itself.

- *Listens for God's Word in prayer and through others.* The lector must accept that the Word proclaimed is not his or her word, but it is God's Word. Listening in prayer is practice in listening to how God wishes the lector to proclaim. Listening through others alerts the lector to the needs of the community, to which God's Word always is a helpful and loving Word.

- *Prays the Scriptures* (lectio divina). The lector reads more of sacred

Scripture than just the Word that will be proclaimed for any given liturgy. The best way to learn to love and cherish the Word of God is to turn to sacred Scripture often to read, reflect, and pray on what God is saying in any given moment. Like Mary, the lector treasures and ponders God's Word in his or her heart (see Luke 2:19).

- *Practices charity and "elegance" in speech.* It is inconceivable that a lector would use unbecoming and harsh language in daily dealings with other people. The same mouth from which comes daily speech is that which utters God's Word.

- *Praises God often and everywhere.* Every proclamation of sacred Scripture inherently praises and thanks God. When praise and thanksgiving are on the tongue of lectors many times throughout the days and weeks, then praise and thanksgiving can be heard in the proclamation of the lector at Mass.

APPROPRIATING THIS SPIRITUALITY

- One concrete behavior I choose to do in my daily living to deepen the spirituality of this ministry for me is . . .

- One concrete action I choose to do to enhance the effectiveness of my ministry is . . .

Spirituality of the Ministry of Extraordinary Minister of Holy Communion

The Being and Doing of the Ministry of Extraordinary Minister of Holy Communion

The extraordinary minister of holy Communion is called "extraordinary" because the ordinary ministers of holy Communion are priests, deacons, and those instituted as acolytes. The *being* of this ministry is to relate as Body of Christ to Body of Christ. The *doing* of this ministry is more than simply distributing consecrated Hosts and Wine. It is giving the risen Christ's Body and Blood to others as heavenly nourishment.

The Role of Extraordinary Minister of Holy Communion

The extraordinary minister of holy Communion is the one who, first and foremost, proclaims by her or his very life belief that she or he is truly the Body of Christ. This minister is gracious (grace-filled, Gift-giving) in distributing holy Communion at Mass and compassionate when bringing holy Communion to the sick and homebound. By the sheer goodness of life, this minister brings Christ's Presence to others—the Blessed Sacrament as well as the risen Presence of Christ in the Church.

Characteristics of the Spirituality of the Ministry of Extraordinary Minister of Holy Communion

- *Strives to be truly present to others.* This ministry is largely about presence: the Presence of the risen Christ in holy Communion, and the presence of the Body of Christ for all we meet. The key to Communion is "communion": striving through presence to be one with another.

- *Believes self and others are truly the Body of Christ and models this in life.* Although Christ's risen Presence in the Blessed Sacrament remains his preeminent Self-giving, that does not make other presences of Christ unimportant. By our baptism and holy lives, we are members of the Body of Christ, and are called to live each day showing forth this divine Presence within us by how we choose to live.

- *Is comfortable looking others "in the eye," with a genuine sharing of self.* In some cultures, it is not appropriate to look another straight in the eye. In our culture, it is, although sometimes this can be difficult. There is a very personal sharing that occurs when two people are "eyeball to eyeball." We see into each other, and there is a genuine sharing of self. Looking another in the eye engenders honesty, trust, and openness. As the Eucharistic minister raises the consecrated Host to the communicant, looking each other in the eye underscores the ministerial, giving, nature of the exchange as well as the dignity of each communicant.

- *Is reverent in body and spirit not only during liturgy but toward others in daily living.* The holy Eucharist deserves our utmost reverence and devotion. When we are reverent in all things we do, we instill a good habit of honoring the dignity of others which carries over into this liturgical ministry.

- *Puts others ahead of self.* The Eucharistic celebration is the continued Self-giving of the risen Christ to us. As Christ gives himself to us, we give ourselves to others. Eucharistic ministers practice self-giving in their daily living when they think of others and put their needs ahead of themselves.

Appropriating This Spirituality

- One concrete behavior I choose to do in my daily living to deepen the spirituality of this ministry for me is . . .

- One concrete action I choose to do to enhance the effectiveness of my ministry is . . .

Spirituality of the Ministry of Liturgical Musician · Music Director · Cantor · Psalmist · Accompanist · Choir

The Being and Doing of the Ministry of Liturgical Musician

Music is often one of the largest parish liturgical ministries. It is not uncommon for a parish to have more than one choir, with at least one of these having a large number of members. The many different musical activities of each liturgy require multiple musicians of differing skills to execute the ministry well. Nevertheless, a common spirituality underlies every musical role. The *being* of the ministry of liturgical musician is to embody the joy and surrender indicative of good liturgy. The *doing* of a liturgical musician is to undertake the important task of promoting full, conscious, and active participation by supporting the assembly in the extra effort that singing requires.

The Role of Liturgical Musician

Through music, these ministers (assembly, psalmist, cantor, choir, music director, presider, accompanist) support the unfolding of the liturgical action and help everyone enter into and respond to that action as the one Body of Christ. Music is essential in promoting full, conscious, and active participation in the liturgy.

Characteristics of the Spirituality of the Ministry of Liturgical Musician

- *Understands a "supporting" role.* The liturgical musician is not a performer, but one who supports others as they enter into the action and movement of the liturgy. To this end, the liturgical musician must surrender self to the action of the liturgy, so that the risen Christ shines through the musician. The liturgical musician must embody the "sound" of surrender.

- *Lives a non-verbal dimension of relationship with God and community.* While most of the music during liturgy involves words, there is also a non-verbal aspect to music: sound, rhythm, volume, even silence. All these non-verbal aspects play into our non-liturgical relationship with God and community. Becoming more attuned to how these occur in daily living helps us be aware of how they occur during liturgy.

- *Recognizes the rhythms of celebration.* Each liturgical celebration has high and low points, and music can help the assembly become more aware of this. The body language, attention, and prayerful attitude of liturgical musicians are noticeable to all present and either call people more deeply into a prayerful celebration or push people out of it. Liturgical musicians carry a serious responsibility.

- *Hears the rhythm of the paschal mystery.* Most importantly, because all music has rhythm, the liturgical musician is primed to enter more deeply into the self-emptying and Life-receiving rhythm of the paschal mystery. This rhythm not only shapes the presentation of liturgical music itself, but also, as liturgical spirituality, shapes the life of the liturgical musician.

- *Sees self as the musical instrument.* The liturgical musician himself or herself is the most important musical instrument, in that liturgical music-making is more than sound; it is the visible surrender of the musician to the liturgical action. When the self surrenders, the music sounds differently. It sounds like the voice of the risen Christ calling to the assembly.

- *Is responsible and dependable.* A great deal of time and detail goes into liturgical music that truly supports the assembly's worship. Being present and on time for practices, coming early for liturgical celebrations to be prepared, knowing what is expected, having order, being appropriately dressed—all these elements and more work together to enable the liturgical musician to function truly as a minister. The same kind of responsibility and dependability in one's daily living help form a good habit that carries over into how one is at worship.

Appropriating This Spirituality

- One concrete behavior I choose to do in my daily living to deepen the spirituality of this ministry for me is . . .
- One concrete action I choose to do to enhance the effectiveness of my ministry is . . .

Spirituality of the Minister of Hospitality · Greeter · Usher

The Being and Doing of the Minister of Hospitality

The word *hospitality* comes from the Latin *hospes* meaning "stranger," "guest." It recalls God's command to care for the stranger because of God's care for Israel during the sojourn in Egypt and the desert. Hospitality is essential to worship because it calls those gathering "home" to be in the Presence of God and surrender their individuality to become one community in Christ. The *being* of this ministry is to embody an invitation to Presence and surrender. The *doing* of this ministry includes welcoming, helping people be comfortable in the sacred space, and being quick to respond to any unexpected needs or accidents.

The Role of Minister of Hospitality

The hospitality ministers welcome the members of the Body of Christ who are gathering for liturgy as sisters and brothers in Christ, assist them with any needs, attend to the good order of the sacred space, and assist other ministers in any way helpful. Therefore, this ministry calls forth from those assembling a deep sense within of their identity as the Body of Christ and "being at home." Hospitality ministers help the assembly members transition from the cares of daily living to surrendering to the majesty and mystery of divine Presence. They help promote unity within the community, help the people gathering to surrender to the Spirit's transforming power, and help the assembly to be Church made visible.

Characteristics of the Spirituality of the Minister of Hospitality

- *Presents a joyful, happy disposition.* The hospitality minister is one who genuinely enjoys meeting and being with people. The hospitality minister is gracious and welcoming when greeting others—at church and in daily living. Nothing is more inviting to those gathering than a genuine, warm smile.

- *Shows genuine care and concern for others.* Love for others and reaching out to them cannot be a once-in-a-while attitude or action. The hospitality minister embodies a caring attitude visible in concern for others.

- *Is "at home" in God's house, prayerful.* The hospitality minister fosters the habit of making God's house his or her own "home." The sacred space must be a comfortable place in which to be, helped by the minister having a prayerful attitude. Even when smiling and greeting people, these actions are done with a prayerful attitude and respect for all. This hospitality is welcoming others to a sacred space for a sacred action.

- *Is hospitable in one's personal life and generous with home and belongings.* Hospitality begins at home. True hospitality signifies gracious generosity that becomes a good habit when it is practiced at home and with one's belongings. The hospitality minister practices at church and in daily living being inclusive of everyone.

- *Is quick to compliment and forgive, surrender and serve, be humble and generous.* True hospitality is a gift of self to others. Anything that gets in the way of genuinely meeting others where they are must be put aside. Past hurts, negative gossip, and bad impressions destroy any real sense of hospitality. Practicing seeing everyone as the beloved of God, helps surrender oneself in humility to serve with joy.

- *Is aware of and attentive to details.* Many unexpected things can happen at liturgy: second and even third collections might be required, items may need to be distributed, someone may get sick, parents might be nervous about their little children misbehaving or babies crying, worship aids might run short, seating might be tight. No matter the unusual circumstances, hospitality ministers need to be aware of what is happening and address any issues, helping make everyone feel comfortable, at ease, and welcome.

APPROPRIATING THIS SPIRITUALITY

- One concrete behavior I choose to do in my daily living to deepen the spirituality of this ministry for me is . . .

- One concrete action I choose to do to enhance the effectiveness of my ministry is . . .

Spirituality of Service Minister · Sacristan · Environment Minister · Janitor · Director/Coordinator of Liturgy · Liturgy Committee

The Being and Doing of Service Minister

When we assemble for liturgy, few of us are aware of all the people who have already contributed to our gathering being comfortable, our space being ready, and our liturgy being celebrated with grace and dignity. Sacristans prepare vestments and vessels and linens and other such tasks, the environment ministers change the way the sacred space looks to draw us into feasts and seasons, janitors repair and clean the space. Then there are members of the liturgy committee who meet regularly to coordinate and plan all things liturgical, and sometimes a parish director of liturgy who sees that everyone and everything is in place. The *being* of this ministry is to personify vision, understanding of liturgy, good order, beauty, and readiness. The *doing* of this ministry is to carry out all the hidden tasks that support liturgy in all its many aspects.

The Role of Service Minister

Service ministers are less visible than many of the other liturgical ministers, but certainly no less important for liturgy to achieve its end. They are often spending hours outside liturgy so actual liturgical celebrations will be optimal in their fruitfulness, beauty, and nobility. They do all the myriad tasks that involve liturgical space, accoutrements, and supplies being in order and available.

THE CHARACTERISTICS OF THE SPIRITUALITY OF SERVICE MINISTER

- *Responsible and dedicated.* The entire liturgical community depends (usually unknowingly) on all the efforts of the various service ministers. If a responsibility is neglected, disaster can occur. Many of the service ministers' tasks are quite repetitive—for example, washing and ironing linens or keeping order in the sacristy—and can, therefore, quickly seem unimportant. Dedicated even to the mundane tasks that aren't very exciting helps liturgy flow more smoothly and beautifully.

- *Generous with time and talent.* Service ministers can sometimes spend long hours doing what needs to be done. This requires both great generosity as well as the necessary talent to do the task well.

- *Maintain balance between ministry and personal life.* Because service ministry can sometimes be so time consuming, it is important that these ministers recognize the demands on them, plan accordingly, and maintain a balance between volunteering at church and the responsibilities of personal life.

- *Sustain a joyful and giving disposition.* Joy is contagious. If service ministers are doing a demanding and time consuming (and sometimes tedious) task, how they treat and encourage each other can make the task seem lighter and get finished quicker.

- *Ability to cooperate in a team effort.* Many tasks of service ministers involve working with other people. The more smoothly and comfortably a team works together, the lighter the task and the quicker will it be finished. Rancor, control issues, non-acceptance of others, pettiness, and demanding one's own way are detrimental to this ministry.

Appropriating This Spirituality

- One concrete behavior I choose to do in my daily living to deepen the spirituality of this ministry for me is . . .

- One concrete action I choose to do to enhance the effectiveness of my ministry is . . .